The Sultan's Fountain

Agnieszka Dobrowolska
Jarosław Dobrowolski

The Sultan's Fountain

An Imperial Story
of Cairo, Istanbul, and Amsterdam

A Netherlands–Flemish Institute in Cairo Edition

The American University in Cairo Press
Cairo • New York

First published in 2011 by
The American University in Cairo Press
113 Sharia Kasr el Aini, Cairo, Egypt
420 Fifth Avenue, New York, NY 10018
www.aucpress.com

Produced as part of a project of the Netherlands–Flemish Institute in Cairo (NVIC) and
funded by the Embassy of the Kingdom of the Netherlands in Cairo. Opinions expressed
in this book are those of the authors, not necessarily those of the NVIC or the sponsor.

Dar el Kutub No. 10368/11
ISBN 978 977 416 523 8

Dar el Kutub Cataloging-in-Publication Data

Dobrowolska, Agnieszka
        The Sultan's Fountain: An Imperial Story of Cairo, Istanbul, and
    Amsterdam/ Agnieszka Dobrowolska and Jaroslaw Dobrowolski.—Cairo: The
    American University in Cairo Press, 2011
            p.   cm.
        ISBN 978 977 416 523 8
        1. Cairo (Egypt)—Description and travel   I. Jaroslaw Dobrowolski
        (jt. auth.)
        2. Islamic architecture
        916.216

1 2 3 4 5 6   14 13 12 11

Designed by Agnieszka Dobrowolska
Printed in Egypt

For Jan

CONTENTS

FOREWORD

Coming in from the noisy streets of Cairo, the cool and quiet sabil room of the sabil–kuttab of Mustafa III is pleasing to the eye and mind. But I did not expect to find myself inside a Dutch 'kitchen' interior, the walls covered in blue and white tiles showing children at play. These rather modest but surprising and unique decorative tiles created a cascade of intriguing questions in my mind, starting with the nature of the connections between the Netherlands and Egypt at the time the sabil was built.

The authors of this wonderfully illustrated book tell us the fascinating story of the sabil and its Dutch tiles. Meant for a wide audience, it explores the histories of the building, its founder, its Dutch tiles, the urban context, and how they are all connected. It furthermore illustrates the conservation project that was initiated by the Netherlands-Flemish Institute (NVIC) and the Embassy of the Kingdom of the Netherlands in Egypt to preserve this remarkable eighteenth-century building and the Dutch cultural treasures that it contains.

The restoration project at the sabil–kuttab was not only a fascinating journey through the art and history of the building. It is also an expression of the commitment by the Embassy and the NVIC to the study and preservation of Egypt's cultural heritage, and the strengthening of the cultural ties between our two countries. I hope this book will inspire you to visit the sabil and discover its charm.

Dr. Kim Duistermaat

PREFACE

This book is intended to guide its readers through landscapes, events, ideas, and people's fates so varied and so far apart that it would seem improbable that they could ever be directly related. Yet they all converge in a single small building in the busy Sayida Zeinab district in Cairo, a building that is exactly 250 years old as this book is being written. Its beautiful architecture alone would be captivating enough, but its blending of different cultures and traditions makes it truly fascinating. Egyptian history going back to the Middle Ages and beyond, the changing fates of the Ottoman empire with its vast holdings on three continents, and the enterprising spirit and technical mastery of the artisans and merchants of Holland—all of these find expression in this building. If our book encourages readers to visit the sabil–kuttab of Sultan Mustafa III and gain an appreciation of how so many diverse influences shaped its gracious architecture, it will have served its purpose.

Acknowledgments

In 2006, Dutch scholar Prof. Hans Theunissen brought the Dutch tiles in the sabil of Sultan Mustafa III to the attention of Dr. Gert Borg, the director of the Netherlands-Flemish Institute in Cairo. This set in motion a chain of events that resulted in the conservation of the building, and in the creation of this book. The funding generously granted by the Embassy of the Kingdom of the Netherlands made the work possible, as did the affiliation of the project to the Netherlands-Flemish Institute. Interest and support of the Institute's directors Dr. Gert Borg and, subsequently, Dr. Kim Duisermaat were essential for the project, as was the efficiency and expediency of its administrative manager Tilly Mulder and all other staff.

The input of Prof. Jason Thompson into the book by editing the text and sharing his insights was priceless. We are also grateful to Donald Benson for his editorial comments and to Prof. Filiz Yenişehirlioğlu of the Başkent University in Ankara who did the illustration research in Turkey, advised in matters of Ottoman history, and located the endowment deed of the building in archives in Ankara. We extend our gratitude to the people and institutions who granted permissions for the illustrations that appear in the book, and especially to *Saudi Aramco World* magazine for allowing us to use the marvellous photographs of our late friend John Feeney. Many others won our appreciation by sharing information on subjects as diverse as the use of Dutch wall tiles in the Baltic States and the family life of Ottoman Sultans.

Most importantly, this book would not have been possible without the work of the people in the conservation team: expert and dedicated professionals, both Egyptian and foreign, whose skilled hands touched virtually every stone in the building during their year-long work.

Finally, the people of the neighborhood are ultimately the ones who made working in the historic Sayida Zeinab area an unforgettable and enriching experience.

A Note on Transliteration

Rendering Arabic words in the Latin alphabet is inherently difficult. No universally accepted system exists, and transliterations are necessarily either imprecise, or legible only to trained Arabists. Peculiarities of the Egyptian dialect of Cairo add to the difficulty. When in addition the Turkish language comes into play, confusion is virtually unavoidable. As a rule, we simplified the British Museum system to use only regular Latin characters, stuck to the (modern) Egyptian version of the language, and used forms that may be familiar to an English-language reader. Therefore, we have Giza, and not "Jizeh," Suleiman, not "Süleyman," and Muhammad, not "Mehmet," regardless of the context. We use Arabic *sabil* for public fountains in Cairo, and Turkish *sebil* for those in Istanbul, because they are not exactly the same thing. A careful reader will inevitably find inconsistencies, for which the authors are solely responsible.

ISTANBUL

Along the Nile, and on the Bosphorus

■

On 24 August 1516 on the plain of Marj Dabiq, a day's march north of Aleppo in Syria, the armies of the Mamluk sultan of Egypt Qansuh al-Ghuri and the Ottoman sultan Selim I met in a decisive battle. The Egyptian Sultanate was long past its glorious days when Mamluk cavalry had defeated the armies of Hulagu Khan in 1260 and checked the advance of the Mongols, thus sparing Cairo the devastation that Baghdad had suffered. The Egyptian capital flourished and became the pre-eminent political, commercial, and artistic center of the Muslim world. By the 1500s, however, the economic foundations of the Mamluk state had been undercut, and its military tactics were becoming obsolete. Yet Qansuh al-Ghuri assembled a formidable army that might have been an equal match for that of Sultan Selim (known in the west as "Selim the Grim"), but the defection of the treacherous governor of Aleppo to the Ottomans sealed the fate of the battle. Qansuh al-Ghuri died of a stroke on the battlefield while preparing for a charge, and the Egyptian troops retreated. It was now only a matter of time for the Ottoman army to enter Cairo, which it did after unsuccessful Mamluk resistance in January 1517. Al-Ghuri's short-lived successor was soon afterward hanged from the Bab Zuwayla city gate. Khayr Bek, the traitor of Marj Dabiq, became the first Ottoman governor of Egypt, and Cairo became an Ottoman provincial capital. As Sultan Selim, who was a distinguished poet as well as a fierce warrior, wrote, "The world is not large enough for two kings."

Above:
Bab Zuwayla city gate in Cairo, with minarets added by the Mamluk sultan al-Mu'ayyad Sheikh in 1415–20.
Right:
A piece of mediaeval textile depicting a Mamluk warrior.

Under Selim's son Suleiman the Magnificent (or Suleiman the Law-Giver, as he is known in the east) the Ottoman Empire reached its peak of might and glory. From its modest origins as a line of nomadic tribal chieftains, the House of Osman had won a world empire that stretched across immense territories on three continents. The Ottoman sultan also asserted his spiritual leadership of all Islam, based on his control of the Islamic holy cities in Arabia and his title of caliph, which was first bestowed on Selim I after he captured Cairo. Suleiman the Magnificent's chief architect Koca Sinan embellished Istanbul with masterpieces befitting an imperial capital and built in the style that came to be considered classical Ottoman architecture.

Opposite page and above:
The mosque of Suleiman the Magnificent in Istanbul, built by
Koca Sinan in 1550–1557, shown in a 16th-century woodcut
based on Melchior Lorich's drawing of 1559, and as it appears
in present-day photographs.

A Mamelouk of Cairo in Egypt.

Cairo, by contrast, was no longer the seat of a sultanate with dominion over its own considerable realm but merely the capital of one of the many provinces in the vast Ottoman Empire that was ruled from Istanbul. A Turkish garrison was stationed at the Citadel of Cairo, and a governor appointed by the sultan in Istanbul oversaw the Egyptian province. The governor was expected to maintain law and order, make sure that the yearly tribute was paid to Istanbul, and maintain the safety of the pilgrimage routes to the Islamic holy cities of Mecca and Medina. But Egypt was an exceptionally important Ottoman province, so Cairo maintained a privileged status. Egypt was the breadbasket of the empire, and the sultans were careful to prevent their governors from building a power base that could eventually enable them to challenge imperial authority. Therefore they appointed them for short terms with promises of even more lucrative positions when they returned to Istanbul. A quick succession of appointments and recalls weakened the position of the governor, who also had to rely on lesser officials who cared more about their own, local agendas than the functioning of the imperial system. Many key offices were increasingly occupied by local Mamluk dignitaries who had the title of Bey.

Opposite page:
A 19th-century engraving of a Mamluk bey.
Above:
At the Citadel of Cairo, the mosque of Muhammad 'Ali was
built in the 19th century over the ruins of the Mamluk sultans'
palace. The lower enclosure was added by the Ottomans.

Khayr Bek was not the only Mamluk official who found his way into the Ottoman administration in Egypt. By the 17th century, other powerful Mamluk warlords who maintained huge households of their own loyal Mamluks had taken control of the crucial offices of Amir al-Hagg (Leader of the Pilgrimage) and Shaykh al-Balad (Governor of Cairo), in addition to other politically important positions. Rarely united, the Mamluk beys were split by their constant competition for power that occasionally erupted into open warfare. The Ottoman governors tried to take advantage of this by allying with one Mamluk faction against another. Only by that means were they able to exercise power. But the Mamluk beys responded by exploiting the rivalries between the different corps that composed the Ottoman garrison so effectively that the governor often could not rely even on his own troops. The power of the beylicate (the twenty-four high-ranking Mamluk military officers appointed to immensely profitable top posts in the administration) grew constantly throughout the 18th century while the authority of the governor diminished.

Opposite page:
Murad Bey, a leading Mamluk dignitary of the late 18th century, depicted in the *Description de l'Égypte* by the Napoleonic expedition.
Above:
The dome of Khayr Bek's mausoleum in Cairo. Although the amir was the first Ottoman governor in Egypt, the architecture is purely Mamluk in style.

The situation was worsened by the increasing tendency of Ottoman sultans to pass their time in sumptuous luxury behind the high walls of the Topkapi Palace in Istanbul, rarely taking an active interest in the internal administration of the provinces. By the early 18th century, their realm was quite different from the dynamic, expanding, and seemingly invincible empire of Mehmet the Conqueror, Selim I, and Suleiman the Magnificent. After Suleiman died in 1566, the empire still had outstanding viziers and military commanders, but very few able sultans. Widespread corruption rotted the administration from within, while the sultans' mothers, wives, and concubines often used their enormous influence to their personal ends, to the detriment of the empire. A pervading conservatism rendered the educational system intellectually stagnant and stifled any attempts at reform. Suleiman the Magnificent's failure to capture Vienna in 1529 was the first signal that the expansion of the Ottoman Empire was not unstoppable. The Ottoman defeat in the second siege of Vienna in 1683 by the coalition forces led by the Polish king Jan III Sobieski marked the point after which the empire steadily contracted, losing one province after another, beginning with most of Hungary in 1699.

Opposite page:
The Sweetmeats Room in the Topkapi Palace, decorated during the reign of Ahmed III, gives a good idea of the luxury and opulence that surrounded Ottoman sultans.
Above:
The monument erected in Warsaw in 1788 to commemorate the victory of Vienna in 1683 shows the Polish king Jan III Sobieski trampling over the defeated Turkish enemies.
Right:
Sultan Mehmet IV, who lost at the second siege of Vienna.

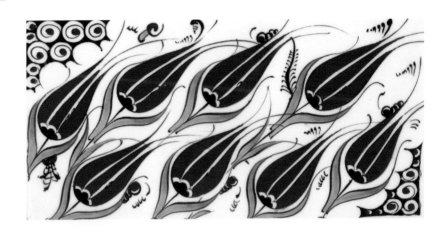

Even as the empire entered a long period of stagnation, 18th-century Istanbul remained a thriving city and a magnificent capital. Wealth continued to pour in from the provinces. The defeats of Ottoman armies were merely sad news from far away. Sumptuous new buildings continued to adorn the city, now in the opulent style of flowing lines, capricious arrangements of volumes, and profuse ornamentation known as the Ottoman Baroque. The city reveled in extravagantly rich festivals organized by the sultan and his ministers. "Let us laugh, let us play, let us enjoy the delights of the world to the full," wrote the court poet to Sultan Ahmed III.

It was during Ahmed III's reign, which lasted from 1703 to 1730, that the passion for tulip flowers, always highly esteemed by the Ottomans, reached the dimension of a mania in Istanbul. Treatises were written about what constituted the beauty of a perfect tulip (twenty different qualities needed to be assessed). Hundreds of varieties were traded, and the most sought-after ones fetched fantastic prices. This was similar to an even more frantic mania for tulips that had gripped Holland some seventy years earlier, resulting in the market for tulip bulbs booming into a monstrously inflated economic bubble that burst in 1637.

Opposite page:
Once established as a decorative motif in the mid 16th-century, tulips continue to inspire pieces like this lid of a contemporary ceramic box.
Above:
Sultan Ahmed III views performances on the Golden Horn from a kiosk in the Topkapi palace. A miniature by the painter Levni from the *Book of Festivities* by the poet Seyyid Hüseyin Vehni, early 18th century.

In Sultan Ahmed III's magnificent gardens in the Abode of Bliss, the Topkapi Palace, extravagant tulip festivals took place annually during the blossom season in April and lasted for two nights, lighted by the full moon and thousands of bright candles that reflected in countless mirrors. Noble guests were required to wear clothes harmonizing with the colors of the tulips in the royal flower-beds; huge tortoises walked around carrying candlesticks on their backs. But Sultan Ahmed's son, who would later become Sultan Mustafa III, could not enjoy the celebrations. At most he could catch a faraway glimpse of the fabulous gardens from the remote palace apartments where he was confined.

Opposite page:
Fireworks and performances at a stately ceremony at Sultan Ahmed III's court. An early
18th-century miniature from the *Book of Festivities*.
Above:
The Baghdad Kiosk at the Topkapi Palace, built in 1639. The stairs next to the pool led down to
Ahmed III's famous tulip gardens.

"Do not expect us to save the world which is being ruined"

Since the ascension to the throne of Suleiman the Magnificent's great-grandson Ahmed I in 1603, the Ottoman Empire had practiced a peculiar way of rearing its future rulers. Previously, every sultan began his reign by having all his brothers executed, a practice sanctioned as law under Mehmet the Conqueror. This ruthless practice removed any prospect of royal siblings usurping the throne or causing civil wars. Why Sultan Ahmed abolished this efficient but cruel legal fratricide is uncertain. Perhaps he found it incompatible with his religion, for Ahmed was a deeply religious man who associated with scholars and pious men. He insisted on enforcing the principles of Islam in his empire. Or perhaps he found it unacceptable that, upon his death, one of his beloved children would have to kill all the others. Ahmed I was a sensitive young man (he ascended the throne as a thirteen-year-old boy and died of typhus aged only twenty-seven) who was fluent in several languages, wrote lyrical poetry under a pen-name, and loved to hunt in the beautiful scenery of the Black Sea coast. It was he who embellished Istanbul with the masterpiece of architecture known as the Blue Mosque.

Hunting was a favourite pastime of rulers and dignitaries throughout the Islamic world. This hunting scene from a modern Iranian miniature is reproduced here double size.

Henceforth, instead of being strangled with silken cords, the ascending sultan's brothers and close relatives were confined to a set of rooms known as Kafes, or the Cage, in the Harem section of the Topkapi palace. They spent their lives under house arrest, in comfort but under constant surveillance and in complete isolation from any events outside the walls of the palace. Suleiman II (1642–1681) summed up this existence when he cried out to court officials who approached him at the Cage: "If my death has been commanded, say so… It is better to die at once than to die a little every day." Only later did he learn that they came to summon him to be elevated to the throne, not for execution. A worse way to prepare a man for ruling a huge and complex empire can hardly be imagined. Yet, for more than 250 years, this was a persisting pattern, and a few of the sultans brought up this way turned out to be able rulers despite their restricted childhoods.

Opposite page:
Sultan Ahmed I in a portrait by Nakkaş Levni in the 18th-century album of Ottoman royal portraits.
Above:
The tiled splendor of the Topkapi Palace. This wall of the Circumcision Pavilion in the Third Court of the palace was decorated for Sultan Ibrahim in 1641.
Right:
Roxelana, the wife of Suleiman the Magnificent, in a 1550 woodcut published by the Venetian Matteo Pagano.

One of them was the father of Mustafa III, Ahmed III, who came to the throne 86 years after the death of the gifted but prematurely deceased Ahmed I, and who reigned over what historians now call "the Tulip Era." During his twenty-seven-year rule he fought a successful war against Russia, defeating Tsar Peter the Great's army. An invasion from the east by Safavid Persia diverted his attention from the Russian front, but that conflict also ended in Ottoman success. He lost Belgrade in the Austro-Turkish war of 1716–18, but his vizier recaptured parts of Greece (including the island of Corfu) from the Venetians. A prosperous economy supported his war efforts and enabled him, a cultured man, to encourage not only tulip cultivation, but also art and literature. The signature piece of Ottoman Baroque architecture, the magnificent sebil (public fountain) that he built in front of the Imperial Gate of the Topkapi Palace next to the Hagia Sophia, remains one of Istanbul's most popular landmarks. The sultan spared no expense on the decoration of the building and had it adorned with lines of verses by the celebrated poet Seyit Vehbi: "The most distinguished among the word-wizards of the age, who strung these pearls on the thread of his verse," according to the poet's own rather immodest words carved in marble on the sebil. Ahmed III spent extravagantly on such buildings and invested heavily in modernization projects, largely inspired from France and Britain, toward whom the sultan leaned because they were at that time natural allies against his Habsburg and Russian enemies.

Opposite page:
Sultan Ahmed III, in a portrait in the series painted by Constantine Kapıdağı during the reign of Selim III and published in London in 1803 as the *Young Atlas*.
Above:
Sultan Ahmet III's *sebil* by the Imperial gate of the Topkapi Palace.

All of this was too much for the unruly and conservative Janissaries. In 1730, they rose in rebellion led by an Albanian upstart called Patrona Halil and marched on Topkapi Palace. The sultan tried to placate the rebels by executing the ministers associated with unpopular policies, but he soon decided that he had no choice but to abdicate. Weeks of turmoil ensued, but if the rioters expected to gain permanent control over the affairs of the state, they were mistaken. The nephew of Ahmed III was taken out of the Cage and made Sultan Mahmud I. He restored order ruthlessly, aided by the highest officials of the empire, who uncharacteristically united against a rebellion that was running out of hand. Patrona Halil and his companions, many of whom had received high offices from the rebel leader, and 7,000 of his supporters were put to death. The tulip-loving Ahmed III spent the remaining six years of his life in the Cage. Young Mustafa, the future Mustafa III, who was thirteen years old and living in the isolation of the Harem during the tumultuous year 1730, probably knew little of the events that ended his father's reign.

Opposite page:
View of Istanbul from the Sultan's secluded Fourth Courtyard
of the Topkapi Palce.
Above:
The *Iftar* Pavilion at the Fourth Courtyard, 1640.

Mahmud I, known as Mahmud the Hunchback, stayed on the throne until his death in 1754. Besides founding important buildings in Istanbul, in 1750 he ordered the construction of a Sufi convent and a handsome sabil–kuttab on the bank of the Khalig al-Misri canal in Cairo, not far from the mosque of Sayida Zeinab. Mahmud I was succeeded by his brother Osman III, whose insignificant reign ended with his death in 1757. The time had finally come for Ahmed III's son to leave the Cage and be girded with the Sword of Osman in a time-honored ceremony in the venerated sanctuary at Eyup by the Golden Horn, in the holiest mosque in Istanbul, founded by Mehmet the Conqueror soon after capturing Constantinople. Thus he became the 26th sultan of the Ottoman Empire as Mustafa III.

Opposite page:
Detail of the sabil–kuttab of Sultan Mustafa III in Cairo.
Above:
The mosque at Eyup in its present form after Sultan Selim III's rebuilding of 1800.
The minarets, a gift of Ahmed III, remain from the earlier building.

Mustafa III was forty years old when he came to the throne, having spent his entire life behind the walls of Topkapi's Harem. His mother, Ahmed III's French wife Amina Mihrishah (sultans' mothers were invariably of foreign origin) died when Mustafa was fifteen. Possibly because of his father's sophistication, he spent his time in the Cage studying literature, medicine, astronomy, and the history of Islam and of the Ottoman Empire. Like his predecessor Ahmed I, he was noted for his piety. Historians agree that Mustafa III saw the urgent need to reform the empire in order to put it on a par with its European rivals, but the opposition from the conservatives in the military and in the religious establishment proved too strong for him to implement any far-reaching changes. Early in his reign, the grand vizier sent an envoy to Vienna with the news of the new sultan's accession to the throne; a similar embassy followed in 1763/64 to the court of Frederick the Great in Berlin. The envoy, Ahmed Resmi Effendi, left detailed accounts of both his embassies that contributed to the growing appreciation within the Ottoman Empire of the need to study European politics. When Resmi relayed Frederick of Prussia's patronizing advice on achieving success in politics, the sultan reportedly smiled and replied, "We desire to achieve this too, but how?" He was probably well aware that corruption and inefficiency had affected his empire too deeply for a quick cure to be available, but he continued to work toward reform.

Opposite page:
Sultan Mustafa III, in a portrait by Constantine Kapıdağı. The scientific instruments and books in the vignette below allude to the sultan's scholarly pursuits.

Above:
By the second half of the 18th century, the weakened Ottoman Empire was increasingly perceived as the powerless Sick Man of Europe. This British caricature of 1772 shows the monarchs of Russia, Prussia, and Austria deciding the fate of Poland to the indifference of the sleeping British King, while the Ottoman sultan Selim III, son of Mustafa III, watches, helplessly bound in chains.

27

In the army, Mustafa III initiated reforms in the artillery and infantry and enlisted an energetic French officer of Hungarian origin, François Baron de Tott, to implement them. De Tott built a new cannon foundry, organized mobile artillery units, and constructed fortifications around the Bosphorus. The sultan even sent de Tott to investigate the possibility of cutting a canal through the Isthmus of Suez, a century before Ferdinand de Lesseps eventually accomplished that feat for the Egyptian khedive Isma'il. Mustafa III also established academies for mathematics, sciences, and navigation as part of his navy. All these attempts at modernization, however, came too little, too late.

Mustafa married Mihrishah Sultan, a native of Genoa and originally named Agnes. With Mihrishah, Mustafa III had a son, the future Sultan Selim III, besides another son and five daughters with other wives. Young Selim was not imprisoned in the Cage, and his father ensured that he received a good education. This effort paid off, because when Selim III finally came to the throne in 1789, he embarked on many momentous reforms that his father had never managed to push through, and although he was assassinated in 1808 before he could see the fruit of his work, the too-long delayed modernization of the empire was set on course.

SULEYMAN IIN ZEVCESI **HURREM SULTAN** FEMME DU SULEYMAN I.

Opposite page:
Entrance to the Suez canal at Port Said, photographed by Francis Frith in
the late 1850s.
Above:
Portraits of women of the sultan's court are extremely rare. Roxelana,
the wife of Suleiman the Magnificent, is an exception. This 18th-century
idealized portrait in the Topkapi Palace is based on contemporary pictures
of the famous Ruthenian.

Aware of his empire's weakness, Sultan Mustafa III avoided war as long as he could, even at the price of territorial losses, while attempting to strengthen and revitalize his realm internally. It was an almost impossible task with corruption and tax abuses rampant, with the intractable Janissaries always ready to rise in rebellion against any reforms, and with provincial administrations that were virtually independent from Istanbul, for the insubordinate Mamluks of Egypt were by no means exceptional. By the late 1760s, however, Russian interference in Polish affairs finally dragged Turkey into war with Russia. The Russians won important victories as they overran the Crimea and territories in the Balkans, while the Russian navy annihilated the Ottoman fleet at Çesme Bay near Izmir in western Anatolia, opposite the isle of Chios. Nevertheless, Mustafa III also achieved enough successes that the conflict continued indecisively. Only after the sultan's death in 1774 did the war end disastrously, forcing the Ottoman Empire to sign the humiliating treaty of Kuchuk Kainarji in the same year.

Opposite page:
The *tughra*, or stylized calligraphic emblem, of Sultan Mustafa III
in the Topkapi Palace.
Above:
The battle of Çesme Bay, in an oil painting by Ivan Konstantinovitch
Aivazovsky, 1848.

In his letters to the Russian monarch Catherine the Great, the French philosopher Voltaire consistently put Mustafa III to ridicule, calling him "fat and ignorant." Whether this resulted more from Voltaire's actual knowledge of Mustafa or from his desire to curry favor with his royal correspondent must remain an open question. But in regard to Mustafa's intelligence, it is worth noting that, like so many Ottoman sultans, he composed poetry. Under the pen-name Djikangir he once wrote:

Do not expect us to save the world which is being ruined;
The bad running of the country has brought about the calamities.
Now everybody at the Imperial Palace is false and base;
Only God, the Merciful and Everlasting, can help us.

Those sad but sharply perceptive lines, though clearly written by a disillusioned and possibly bitter man, hardly sound like a pronouncement of an "ignorant" person.

Yet, while Sultan Mustafa had many good reasons to be disillusioned and frustrated in politics and reform, he could at least find satisfaction in adorning Istanbul and other cities with beautiful structures, continuing the Ottomans' passion for building that had never abated since the glorious days of Suleiman the Magnificent and his architect Koca Sinan.

Opposite page:
This British caricature of 1787 shows Mustafa III's son Sultan
Selim III in a futile attempt to fight the invincible Catherine the
Great.
Above:
François-Marie Arouet, better known under his pen name Voltaire
at Frederick of Prussia's court at Sanssouci. An engraving by
Pierre Charles Baquoy, ca. 1795.

33

Mustafa the Builder

That the Ottoman rulers would become enthusiastic patrons of monumental architecture was by no means predictable, because the Ottomans never completely shed traditions that were deeply rooted in their nomadic origins. One indication of this was their widespread use of tents for different purposes. The rulers erected veritable tent-cities and tent-palaces during their military campaigns and for imperial festivities. These were designed both to provide comforts matching those of the permanent palace and to project the message of power and splendor through their magnificence and sheer size. Six hundred camels were needed to carry the royal tents of Mehmet IV in the late 17th century.

But the Ottomans, who symbolically and emotionally valued their nomadic legacy, also had a passion for leaving their mark in bricks and stones. When their young empire expanded, they left behind a trail of architectural creations. Modest beginnings by the early rulers in Söğüt, Bilecik, and Iznik in the early 14th century had evolved into the huge and sophisticated mosques, religious colleges, and commercial buildings of Bursa, Manisa, and Edirne by the early 15th century.

But it was only with the conquest of Constantinople in 1453 that the Ottoman sultans found the setting in which their building ambitions could reach a truly imperial scale, culminating in the 16th century with structures that were, and still are, the wonders of the world. The sultan's (and so the state's) chief architect was an important official within the highly regulated structure of the empire, and he was kept busy. A list of buildings erected by Suleiman the Magnificent's architect Koca Sinan includes about 120 entries; many were giant multipurpose complexes. More than 40 still stand in Istanbul alone.

In overall design, the Ottoman architects were concerned with balancing the open, semi-enclosed, and enclosed spaces of courtyards, porticoes, and interiors; with achieving both unity and variety in spacious dome-covered halls; and with combining a building's parts of different geometric shapes into a harmonious whole. In interior decoration, ceramic wall-tiles reigned supreme. Virtually all of the tiles were produced in the kilns of Iznik in northwestern Anatolia, a city that was an important centre of pottery production long before the Ottoman conquest.

Previous page:
Sultan Suleiman the Magnificent in his tent during a military campaign. Illustration in a manuscript of 1558, now in the Topkapi Museum.
Opposite page:
The Suleimaniye Mosque, built in Istanbul by Suleiman the Magnificent's architect Koca Sinan in 1550–1557, photographed by Pascal Sebah around the year 1900.
Above:
The Mosque of Sultan Ahmed I in Istanbul (known as the Blue Mosque), built by architect Mehmet Ağa in 1609–1616, sums up the achievements of the classical period of Ottoman architecture.

The Iznik potters drew on two sources of technological and artistic inspiration. One was the long and rich tradition of Islamic ceramics. The other was Chinese porcelain, a luxury much sought after and often imitated in the Islamic world.

But the potters of Iznik and, since the time of Mehmet the Conqueror, the royal design atelier in Istanbul that provided them with patterns were not mere imitators. They soon produced outstanding pieces of original and sophisticated design. By the time of Suleiman the Magnificent they were using a palette of seven different pigments in a technologically complex process of underglaze-painted decoration. This is remarkable, because few pigments are suitable for such use; most colors would melt and run in the high temperature of the kiln, blurring the designs. Because of the scale of imperial commissions, wall-tiles dominated Iznik production. More than 20,000 pieces were used to adorn Sultan Ahmed I's Blue Mosque (finished in 1616), but this was the last great commission for the Iznik kilns. Only about twenty were still working in 1620, and the quality of their output had declined drastically.

Opposite page:
The Blue Mosque, seen from the Hippodrome in Istanbul.
Above:
The interior of the Blue Mosque.

By the mid-18th century, reigning over a troubled and weakened empire, Sultan Mustafa III could only dream of matching the architectural achievements of the Ottoman glory days in magnitude. Still, he was a dedicated patron of architecture. There is a touchingly human aspect to the fact that as soon as he began his reign in 1757, he ordered the erection of a mosque commemorating his late mother, Emina Mihrishah. The dome of the mosque, in the fashionable Ottoman Baroque style of the day, sits graciously on a hilltop above the Üsküdar district in Istanbul's Asian section, overlooking the mouth of the Bosphorus and the Sea of Marmara. The fine marble mosaic inlay decorating the internal gallery in the mosque and the imported Chinese tiles used elsewhere in the building indicate that good-quality, locally produced wall tiles were no longer available.

Opposite page and above:
The Ayazma Mosque in Üsküdar comissioned by Mustafa III to
comemorate his mother, ca. 1900 and nowadays.

Though modest in size, the Sultan's own imperial mosque, the Laleli Cami, was a high achievement of Ottoman Baroque architecture. Here too rare marbles, onyx, jasper, and lapis lazuli combine
in fine inlays, but wall-tiles are absent. Like all other imperial foundations, the mosque was at the center of a huge multifunctional
complex including educational and charitable institutions, as well
as commercial establishments that paid for its upkeep. Although
some of the Laleli Cami complex has been destroyed, the remains
include the sultan's rather somber domed mausoleum and a sebil,
or public fountain. The latter is a handsome, opulently decorated,
round-fronted structure with a marble-clad façade and elaborate
bronze window grilles.

Opposite page:
The Laleli Mosque ca, 1900.
Above:
Interior of the Laleli Mosque dome.

When a catastrophic earthquake devastated Istanbul in the early morning of 22 May 1766, Sultan Mustafa III reportedly took much interest in the relief work and used his personal wealth to help the victims. His freshly constructed Laleli Mosque was heavily damaged and needed to be restored. Moreover, the Fatih Mosque built by Mehmet the Conqueror had collapsed. In an ironic twist of fate, it was its rebuilding by Mustafa III, a disillusioned champion of belated reforms for a weakened empire, that gave this monument—a symbol of Ottoman power, conquest, and rule over the Bosphorus—its present-day appearance. Tellingly, the architecture was not in the style that was current at that moment, but instead consciously followed the examples of the grand classical manner of the Ottoman days of might and glory. The sultan also erected buildings outside the capital. A mosque is attributed to him on the island of Rhodes, and by 1759 his attention had focused on Cairo.

Opposite page:
Sebil built by Mustafa III in Istanbul.
Above:
The Fatih mosque in Istanbul.

CAIRO

Architecture as a Message

■

Just nine years after his cousin Sultan Mahmud I built a taqia (a Sufi convent) and a sabil–kuttab in Cairo, Mustafa III decided to follow suit. We will probably never learn the details of his reasoning, but the sultan's motives for erecting the building, for choosing its location, and for deciding how it should look can easily be imagined.

With the power of the Mamluk beylicate overshadowing the authority of the Ottoman governor, it was natural for the sultan to be eager to mark Cairo with a solid, lasting physical symbol of his suzerainty over the Egyptian province. The priority that he assigned to this project—and not surprisingly, considering Egypt's importance for the empire—is evident from the fact that he embarked on the task soon after ascending to the throne. Mustafa had good reason for haste. Just six years earlier, and only three years after Sultan Mahmud had built his sabil–kuttab in Cairo, Ibrahim Agha Mustahfizan, a local Mamluk bey, erected a no less sumptuous one, "a fountain pure and scented with flowers, whose beauty is perfect," as an inscription on the façade still proclaims, although little remains of the once splendid building. Mustafa wanted to trump that regional architectural statement with one that asserted his imperial authority in Cairo. But why did he decide to do that by erecting a building quite different from anything built at the time in Istanbul?

The sabil–kuttab of Sultan Mustafa III in May 2009.

In a feature found almost only in Cairo, sabils, the public fountains that distributed free drinking water as a charity, were combined in a single building with kuttabs, elementary schools. Initially founded by medieval Mamluk sultans as parts of larger religious complexes, after the Ottoman conquest of 1517 these sabil–kuttabs were increasingly built as free-standing structures by government dignitaries or exceptionally wealthy people, quite often women. Sabil–kuttabs were a much-welcome charity in a city where well water was brackish, and drinking water had to be brought from the Nile by water-carriers. In addition to the religious merits of the charitable foundations, they commemorated the founder's name or that of a beloved deceased person while advertising the wealth, social status, and political importance of the founder. By the middle of the 18th century, Cairo had many sumptuous sabil–kuttabs founded by the local rich and powerful, but few structures that proclaimed the authority of the Ottoman sultan in architectural terms. It appears that Mustafa III wanted to build a magnificent sabil–kuttab in the city that would outdo the local beys on their own turf and address the sultan's Egyptian subjects in the language of architectural forms that they knew and understood well. This can also explain why the building in Cairo is larger than Mustafa III's sebil in Istanbul, and is in fact larger than most sebils in the imperial capital.

Opposite page:
Water carriers drawn by E.W.
Lane in the 1830s.
Right:
Sabil–kuttab attached to the
mosque of Amir Inal al-Yusufi,
1392.
Below:
Detail of the sabil–kuttab of
Lady Ruqaya Dudu, 1761.

If the reason for erecting the building was to send a strong message about the sultan's authority in Egypt, the choice of location was its logical consequence. When Mustafa III's sabil–kuttab was constructed, it faced a canal whose waters (in the months when it was full) could reflect its ornate façade. Today it faces a multi-lane urban thoroughfare packed with traffic and ending at a city square that is as chaotic as it is crowded and noisy. But the area was also important and busy during the 18th century. Across the canal, at the other end of the Lions' Bridge, stood the mosque that had for centuries been venerated because it is located where Sayida (Lady) Zeinab, the granddaughter of the Prophet Muhammad, was believed to be buried. It had become a major pilgrimage destination with an annual festival that attracted innumerable crowds of people from Cairo and afar. This was a perfect location to broadcast the sultan's message of authority.

Moreover, distributing free drinking water at religious festivals was an established way of demonstrating one's piety, because offering water to the thirsty has always been a highly regarded act of charity in Islam. By placing a building designed to offer free drinking water next to the venerated mosque, the sultan reminded his Egyptian subjects that he was not only their temporal ruler, but also the caliph of Islam, whom they should consider their spiritual leader.

52

85 CAIRO. — Mosque Seyideh Zenab. — LL.

Top:
The mosque of Sayida Zeinab on an early 20th-century postcard.
Bottom:
The Khalig al-Misri canal, from the *Description de l'Égypte*, 1828.

"God has purified you,
O Sister of al-Husayn"

It is easy to understand why Sayida Zeinab has always enjoyed such veneration among Egyptian Muslims. She was the granddaughter of the Prophet Muhammad by his daughter Fatima and 'Ali, the fourth and last Rightly Guided Caliph. Born in AD 628, six years after Muhammad's flight from Mecca to Medina that marked the beginning of the Islamic era, she was given her name by the Prophet himself. She was with her brother Husayn at Karbala in present-day Iraq when he was killed in the battle against his overwhelmingly strong Umayyad enemies, who seized the caliphate from the descendants of Sayida Zeinab's father, causing a rift that still divides Islam into the Sunnis and the Shi'a. Zeinab, then fifty-two years old, was arrested and sent to Damascus by the victors. Released by Caliph Muawiyya, she moved to Medina but had to leave because family connections kept her embroiled in the controversy over the succession. She then traveled to Egypt and settled in Fustat, the new capital that the conquering Arabs had established forty years earlier. Fustat was already developing rapidly into an important and prosperous commercial center from which the modern metropolis of Cairo would eventually evolve. Sayida Zeinab died there in 681 after a year-long stay.

The entrance to the mosque of Sayida Zeinab, 2009.

The memory of Lady Zeinab held special significance for the Fatimids, who conquered Egypt in 969 and laid out a new city called al-Qahira just north of Fustat. The Fatimids were Isma'ili Shi'a Muslims who held Sayida Zeinab's father 'Ali in the highest respect; the very name of the dynasty derived from the name of her mother. In the speeches that Sayida Zeinab made after the battle of Karbala the Isma'ilis saw the origin of the preaching of Islamic values (*da'wa*), an element that was central to their beliefs and practices. The Fatimids had a *mashhad*, a commemorative shrine, built next to Sayida Zeinab's tomb. A mashhad was a peculiarly Fatimid type of building where prayers could be said next to a tomb of a saintly or important person. Cairo contains a number of shrines where such persons are venerated; notably, many of those persons from the early days of Islam were women. Several Fatimid mashhads have been preserved in Egypt; their simple but captivating architecture masterfully exploits the interplay between open, semi-enclosed, and interior spaces. The most important shrines have been altered and rebuilt many times over because the veneration of saintly individuals continued unabated when Egypt reverted to Sunni Islam after Salah al-Din Yusuf ibn Ayyub (known as Saladin in the west) put an end to the Fatimid dynasty in 1171. This was also the case with the mosque of Sayida Zeinab.

Opposite page:
In Aswan, the mausoleum of Aga Khan III, the leader of Isma'ili Shi'a Muslims, follows the architectural tradition of the Fatimids.

Above:
The *mashhad* of al-Guyushi still commands the skyline of Cairo from its location on top of the Muqqatam hills more than 900 years after it was built in 1085.

Details of the building are known only since 1549, when an earlier mosque of Sayida Zeinab was rebuilt by 'Ali Pasha, the Ottoman governor. The building was then reconstructed in the middle of the 18th century by a great patron of architecture Abd al-Rahman Katkhuda Bey, the leader of the Qazdughliya Mamluk faction. This illustrates how within two hundred years real power had passed from the Ottoman governors to the local notables. The mosque was repaired again in 1798 but left incomplete because of Napoleon Bonaparte's invasion. Then Muhammad 'Ali Pasha began rebuilding it in the early 19th century, and the work was finished under the rule of Abbas I in 1859. Khedive Tawfiq ordered a total rebuilding of the mosque, which was completed in 1884 in the neo-Mamluk style. King Farouk added an annex in 1942, and the mosque was again enlarged in the 1990s. So much attention to the shrine over the centuries testifies to its sustained popular veneration by the Egyptian people and to the support it received from the ruling classes.

Many Egyptians—especially women—consider Sayida Zeinab a saint, and visit the mosque seeking *baraka* (blessing) in matters of fortune and health. The British traveler and careful observer E.W. Lane aptly described in his influential book *Manners and Customs of the Modern Egyptians* how this custom of visiting saintly persons' sanctuaries was practiced during the 1820s and 1830s:

> *The Egyptians occasionally visit these and other sanctuaries of their saints, either merely with the view of paying honour to the deceased, and performing meritorious acts for the sake of these venerated persons, which they believe will call down a blessing on themselves, or for the purpose of urging some special petition, as for restoration of health, or for the gift of offspring, &c.; in the persuasion that the merits of the deceased will insure a favourable reception of the prayers which they offer up in such consecrated places.*

Top:
The mosque of Sayida Zeinab.
Bottom:
Worshipers at the shrine of Sayida Zeinab.

If Lane's book is still in print more than 170 years after its original publication, it is partly because many such customs remain unchanged. A character in the story "The Lamp of Umm Hashim," written by the renowned Egyptian author Yahia Haqqi and set in mid-twentieth century Cairo, pleads to Sayida Zeinab:

> *God has purified you, has sustained you and put you down in His garden, and your heart is compassionate. If the sick, the defeated and the broken have not sought you, then who else should they seek? . . . O Sister of al-Husayn!*

The people of Cairo continue to visit the tombs of venerated people and seek protection and advice, just as when Yahia Haqqi wrote sixty years ago how "men and women of the family to obtain blessings from visiting the family of the Prophet would be pushed forward as they approached the entrance to the Mosque of Sayyida Zeinab." When Ryszard Kapuściński (hailed by *Der Spiegel* magazine as "the greatest reporter in the world"), who could so often perceive the hidden sense of scenes he encountered, visited Egypt in 1999, he directed his steps to such shrines, striving to understand how the spiritual power behind them defined the spirit of Cairo.

Above:
Pilgrims to Sayida Zeinab shrine enjoy a meal in front of the mosque.
Left:
Cover of a popular edition of Yahia Haqqi's *The Lamp of Umm Hashim*.

61

The mosque of Sayida Zeinab is one of the most frequented shrines in the city. People refer to her as Umm al-Awagez, the Mother of the Destitute, or as Umm Hashim, Mother of the House of the Prophet. In popular Cairene imagination Sayida Zeinab is perceived as the Mother of Egypt, and all powers of motherhood are attributed to her. There is a powerful symbolic aspect of her cult among both the popular and literate classes of Egypt. Egyptians associate her with their country and the Nile, and turn a deaf ear to some historians' doubts whether the mosque is indeed the place of her burial. The whole administrative district of the city where the mosque is located is named after Sayida Zeinab. In Cairo, people often use names quite different from official designations of various places in the city, but in this case there is perfect unanimity: this is the Sayida Zeinab area both for the officials in the city hall and for the person in the street.

The popular manifestations of Sayida Zeinab's veneration culminate in the celebration of her moulid, a festival celebrated on a saint's birthday. E.W. Lane, always eager to observe different aspects of Egyptian culture, attended the moulid of Sayida Zeinab in early 1830s:

> *I have just been to visit it, on the last day or great day of the festival. . . . The door of the sacred enclosure was open; but I had been told that only women were allowed to enter, it being regarded in the same light as a harem: so I contented myself with making the circuit; which, owing to crowding of the visiters, and there being but a very narrow space between three sides of the bronze enclosure and the walls of the apartment, was rather difficult to accomplish.*

Left:
The minaret of Sayida Zeinab mosque decorated for the moulid in 2008.
Below:
A fire breather and a rope walker at a moulid in Cairo.

Page 65:
Happy crowds at a moulid in Cairo.

This is also the first impression of anybody attending the festival in modern times: the overwhelming multitude of the innumerable crowds. Part pilgrimage, part carnival, part mystical Islamic ceremony, this is one of the most important and most frequented of some 3,000 moulids held in Egypt each year.

Sayida Zeinab's moulids are great social levelers. All the usual boundaries of class and wealth are removed as doctors and lawyers mix with manual laborers, city professionals with peasant farmers, street performers with local officials. Islam's usually strict rules of gender segregation for religious events are also suspended for the moulid. On the Big Night, hundreds of thousands of revelers come from all over Cairo and from all across Egypt. Thousands of families sleep inside the mosque and in brightly colored tents put up in the surrounding alleyways. They also cook and eat there, huddled around gas lamps and kerosene stoves. In colorful marquees members of Sufi brotherhoods celebrate. Followers of different orders (*tariqa*, literally: road, path) perform the *zikr* ritual, chanting the name of God over and over again, at an ever increasing tempo. Some achieve a trance-like state. A moulid is also about *khidma*, or service, and many Sufi orders build tents where they offer free food to the poor.

The moulid of Sayida Zeinab is also a great popular feast and a giant popular fair, a place of infinite variety and surprise. Performers and snake-charmers display their skills; numerous stalls offer all kind of goods for sale: shoes, T-shirts, and ladies' purses not-quite-perfectly imitating expensive and fashionable brands; plastic toys and party hats; and drinks, sweets, and snacks. The amplified noise of loudspeakers can be heard from far away.

In spite of the inevitable commercialization, the moulid is ultimately a journey of personal devotion for those who attend it – an expression of love of God and for one's fellow pilgrims. A moulid is also about contemplation, and the spiritual focus of the festival is the mosque where Sayida Zeinab is believed to be buried. At the saint's tomb, devotees take a quiet moment away from the frenzied activity outside to contemplate God, Zeinab's life, and their own spirituality.

In 2009, when these pages were written, the authorities banned the moulids in Egypt in order to avoid huge gatherings of people in the face of the threat of swine flu epidemics. Will this mark a permanent end of the festivals that for generations have brought together people coming to express their beliefs and traditions in joyful celebrations, paying no heed to any fundamentalist or political interpretations of religion? If indeed they disappear in our lifetime, Egypt will have lost something important.

Top:
A muezzin calling to prayer in Cairo.
Bottom:
A devoted pilgrim prays at the shrine of Sayida Zeinab.

The Canal

While the proximity of the venerated shrine of Sayida Zeinab was undoubtedly a factor in the choice of location for Sultan Mustafa's sabil–kuttab, the canal on the bank of which it was built was another. A practical aspect was involved: the huge underground cisterns in which water was stored in Cairene sabils were filled once a year with Nile water from water-skins carried by pack animals. This was done in the time of the Nile inundation, when the canal filled with water; the proximity of the canal was obviously an advantage.

But the canal-side location offered other advantages. As Cairo prospered commercially in spite of any political calamities, the city expanded southward along the canal. Many luxurious residences, commercial establishments, and religious buildings were constructed along its banks and around the seasonal lakes connected to it, away from the crowded medieval center. The lakes fed by the Khalig al-Misri canal filled up with water when the Nile swelled with the annual flood in summer. The cutting of the dike at the mouth of the canal when the inundation began was celebrated well into the 19th century with what was probably Cairo's largest yearly festival. As the Nile waters receded, the dike would be closed, and the lakes remained filled with water for as long as eight months.

Top:
The cistern under the sabil–kuttab of Sultan Mustafa III, cleaned in 2009.
Bottom:
Cutting of the Dike ceremony as depicted in the *Description de l'Égypte*.

As Caroline Williams wrote in her excellent *Islamic Monuments in Cairo: the Practical Guide* (AUC Press 2008): "between 1650 and 1755 this area east of the canal and near Birkat al-Fil was *the* fashionable place to build." Around 1700, a European living in Cairo observed: "The most beautiful houses in Cairo are situated around [Birkat al-Fil]. There is not a day when fireworks are not set off and music is not heard." In 1735, Benoît de Maillet, the French consul in Cairo, described Birkat al-Fil (Elephant Pond): "Nothing is more pleasant than this place filled with water during eight months of the year, while during the remaining months, it turns into a perfumed garden."

As the area around Birkat al-Fil close to the Sayida Zeinab mosque filled up, the rich and powerful of Cairo took up residence around another lake on the other side of the canal: the Ezbekiya, "a sizeable place which is a marketplace, a promenade, or a lake in this city, depending on the season," as the Polish traveler Władysław Wężyk viewed it in 1839. He continued:

> *It's evening already…How different is Izbikie from what we saw in the morning! Thousands of tiny wicker chairs, as in the Tuilleries, and on them sit Turks, Arabs, Copts, Europeans—smoking pipes, drinking coffee, and enjoying the beautiful view; and soon, also pleasant coolness. Others stroll around. Even ladies' hats can be seen. . . . This city square with a lake at its centre*

Top:
Mansions lining the Khalig al-Misri canal in a lithograph in *Egypte Moderne* by A. F. Lemaitre, 1821
Bottom:
Southern shore of the Ezbekiya lake, from the *Description de l'Égypte*.

circled by a street lined with rare palm trees . . . owes all its beauty to Nature itself and to the trait of Oriental appeal that it reflects even as its lake reflects the rays of the setting sun.

The Frenchman Savary had earlier observed how at night, "the palaces of the beys are lit by lamps of different colors. Several thousand boats with lights hanging from their masts produce an ever-shifting pattern of illumination."

The lake was filled in by Muhammad 'Ali Pasha in the first half of the 19th century and turned into a formal garden. It was redesigned under Khedive Isma'il in 1870 when 5000 gas lamps were installed to light it at night. Nowadayws, although bisected by a street and encroached upon by buildings, the still beautiful Ezbekiya garden is one of the few green spaces in the extremely dense downtown area of Cairo.

Opposite page and top:
The western and northwestern shores of the Ezbekiya lake in the *Description de l'Égypte.*
Bottom:
The Ezbekiya Gardens today, with the equestrian statue of Ibrahim Pasha by Charles Cordier, erected in 1872.

The Khalig al-Misri canal was an ancient one. Part of a waterway that once linked the Red Sea with the Nile, and thus with the Mediterranean, it was begun about 600 BC by King Necho II of the 26th Dynasty. Necho was the first Egyptian king to establish a permanent navy, and the canal, in addition to its value for commerce, was intended to permit Egyptian triremes (manned by Greek sailors) to operate on both seas. After the Persian king Cambyses conquered Egypt, putting an end to the 26th Dynasty, his son Darius I completed the work on the canal, providing another example to show that the people of what is now Iran were not just the aggressive and destructive occupiers they were portrayed as by the ancient Greeks.

The canal continued to run its course through what is now Cairo during the Roman Empire. Recent archaeological work in Old Cairo, the site of the Roman fortress called Babylon, revealed massive stone revetments at the mouth of the canal dating from the reign of the Emperor Trajan in the early 2nd century AD. Just three years after the Arab conquest of Egypt in 640 the conqueror and then governor 'Amr Ibn al-'As ordered the re-cutting of the canal that had meanwhile fallen into disuse. It was repeatedly repaired in later centuries after periods of neglect, although in Mamluk and later times the canal was used only for irrigation, not for long-distance

Top:
Painting of an Egyptian ship in the tomb of Menna in Luxor, ca 1390 BC.
Bottom:
A lion-shaped stone mooring post from the mouth of the Roman canal, recently discovered at the Babylon site in Old Cairo.

75

navigation. In the 14th century, Sultan al-Nasir Muhammad connected it to the Nile farther north of its original opening, which had been rendered inconvenient by the continuous westward shift of the Nile's course. The resulting change in topography is still discernible and explains the street pattern in the Sayida Zeinab area, which might otherwise seem odd. The sabil–kuttab of Mustafa III stands in a curving line of buildings that follows the bend of the canal where it once turned toward the Nile.

The Khalig al-Misri canal was filled in at the end of the 19th century, when advances in medicine demonstrated the connection between stagnant water and disease. The former canal's bed was later widened to form a broad thoroughfare in the crowded mediaeval city. This involved extensive demolitions, not unlike Baron Haussmann's in Paris. The Comité de Conservation des Monuments de l'Art Arabe, formed in 1882, transferred a number of historic buildings that stood on the edge of the canal to different locations, but neither the sabil of Mustafa III nor the mosque of Sayida Zeinab was directly affected. The avenue was initially named Khalig al-Misri Street after the canal whose course it ran; it was changed to Port Said Street in 1958. In Cairo, old customs die hard: more than sixty years later in 2009, some commercial companies still advertise on the Web with addresses on the Khalig al-Misri Street.

Top:
The sabil–kuttab of Sultan Mustafa III in its urban context today.
Bottom:
The sabil of Umm Husain Bey, 1851, moved by the Comité to a new location.

One Building,
Different Histories

When the present mosque of Sayida Zeinab was built in 1884, enlarged in 1942, and again enlarged in the 1990s, it was always in the neo-Mamluk style. This says much about how the style has long been perceived as the quintessence of Cairo, and as an expression in bricks and stone of Egyptian national identity.

Mamluk architecture, born in Cairo and distinctive of the city, defined the skyline of the Egyptian capital for centuries. Built from local limestone and skilfully decorated by local craftsmen, it influenced buildings erected long after the Mamluk sultanate was terminated in 1517. In spite of the richness and variety of the style, the architectural vocabulary of Mamluk buildings was highly standardized. Windows placed in stalactite-crowned recesses in the façades, portals recessed under trefoil semi-domes, stone domes decorated with geometric or stylized floral patterns carved in structural stone were among the elements from which the Cairene builders of Mamluk times were able to create infinitely variable compositions. Even today, the skyline of Cairo's old city owes its unmistakeable, fairytale-like silhouette to Mamluk architecture with its floral crenellations over the façades, countless domes, and elegant Mamluk minarets, divided in three stories, with richly carved shafts and (since the early 15th century) supporting colonnaded pavilions surmounted by onion-shaped bulbs.

Mamluk domes of the Southern Cemetery seen against the Muhammad `Ali Mosque at the Citadel.

The sabil–kuttabs well exemplify the variety within uniformity that is typical of Mamluk architecture and testify to its persistence after the demise of the Mamluk sultanate. From the late 15th century on, though often built as free-standing buildings instead of parts of larger religious complexes as was the case before, sabil–kuttabs changed very little in their appearance throughout the 16th, 17th, and early 18th centuries. On the ground floor, large rectangular windows were approached over a few stone steps by the passers-by who would receive through the openings in bronze or iron window grilles a cup of water that was fetched from a huge underground cistern. Above, marble columns supported pointed arches to form an open loggia where boys would receive their instruction, sitting

Opposite page:
The skyline of Cairo: invariably fascinating for travelers, authors, and artists for many centuries.
Above and right:
Mamluk domes and minarets are a trademark of Cairene architecture.

on the floor in the Turkish manner around the teacher and writing with chalk on small tablets. Wide wooden awnings supported by elaborate brackets provided shade; a decorated recessed portal housed the entrance door. The decoration carved in the structural stone of the façades was entirely Mamluk in its forms. The primary motifs were knotted double moldings, rows of "stalactite" muqarnas niches, and joggled voussoirs of the flat arches that formed lintels, just as in earlier buildings of the Mamluk period. Other carry-overs from the Mamluk tradition were the forms of geometric mosaic patterns of multicolor marble floors, marble dado lining to the lower parts of the walls, decorative woodwork forming geometric patterns on doors and shutters, and painted and carved wooden ceilings that adorned the interiors.

Opposite page:
Shadow and light on a façade of the sabil–kuttab of Sultan Qaitbay built in 1479.
Above:
Another sabil–kuttab of Sultan Qaitbay in al-Azhar area, built in 1477 and set in a corner of a huge commercial complex.

SABIL KUTTAB RUQAYYA DUDU

Many of these Mamluk motifs can be found in the sabil–kuttab of Sultan Mustafa III, which was built in a hybrid style that combined this deeply rooted local tradition with influences from Istanbul. The Istanbul-inspired aspect of the building is the Ottoman Baroque style that prevailed in the imperial capital at the time. It belonged to a completely different tradition from the Mamluk, but it had already begun to influence architecture in Cairo when Sultan Mustafa III came to the throne.

Over time, builders in Cairo had gradually begun to adopt some elements of Ottoman style. The first to change were the minarets. Although Mamluk-style minarets were sometimes still built in Ottoman Egypt, the characteristic pencil-like shape of the Ottoman minaret became almost omnipresent. Not incidentally, soon after the conquest of Cairo, the Ottoman governors ordered Turkish-style minarets to be built in the most visible and prestigious locations—on the Citadel, at the edge of former Mamluk parade grounds, on the city's main thoroughfare—thus making a strong visual statement of Ottoman suzerainty over the country. Iznik wall-tiles soon found their way into lunettes over windows and doors and accentuated other important points on the façades, but

Opposite page:
The sabil–kuttab of Ruqaya Dudu (1761), a hybrid design combining motifs of Mamluk and Ottoman architecture.
Top:
The pencil-like Ottoman minaret of Messih Pasha (1575) and the Muhammad `Ali Mosque (1848) at the Citadel.

Page 86: Ottoman wall tiles installed in 1652 in the Blue Mosque in Cairo.
Page 87: The sabil–kuttab of 'Abd al-Rahman Katkhuda (1744).

unlike in Istanbul, they were rarely used in huge quantities as wall panels decorating interiors. (The mosque of Amir Aqsunqur in Darb al-Ahmar, known as the Blue Mosque on the account of the magnificent tile panels that decorate some of its interiors since 1652, is among the exceptions.) Typically Turkish motifs like stylized cypress trees and naturalistic flowers were increasingly used alongside geometric patterns of Mamluk lineage.

The breakthrough came with the works of architecture—both new buildings and restorations of old ones, including the mosque of Sayida Zeinab—commissioned in the mid-18th century by 'Abd al-Rahman Katkhuda, the enormously wealthy and influential leader of the Qazdughli faction of the Mamluks. The sabil–kuttab that he built in the prestigious location at the heart of medieval Cairo where its main thoroughfare forks into two streets leading to two Fatimid city gates in the Northern Walls is still a major landmark. It demonstrates very well the characteristics of the peculiar combination of local tradition and Ottoman Baroque that 'Abd al-Rahman Katkhuda's buildings introduced to Cairo.

The windows of the three façades of the sabil of 'Abd al-Rahman Katkhuda are arched and set into arched recesses. This multiplication of curves gives the building a sense of dynamic fluidity so typical of the Ottoman Baroque style. The white marble of the façade includes carvings of naturalistically rendered flowers. The peonies, asters, and chrysanthemums are motifs of Far Eastern origin that had become very popular in the Ottoman capital. The interior is covered with blue and green Iznik-type wall tiles. Still, many elements of Mamluk origin are present in the building. First of all, there is a loggia of the kuttab over the sabil, a uniquely Cairene combination not to be found in Istanbul. Where capricious lines of curvilinear cornices would be seen in Istanbul, in 'Abd al-Rahman Katkhuda's building the kuttab is shadowed by overhanging eaves on wooden brackets, much like its Mamluk predecessors. Many decorative motifs, like the knotted double moldings, also continue the local tradition, and the elaborate entrance porch in the side façade is completely within the Mamluk architectural idiom. The sabil–kuttab of Sultan Mustafa III combines Mamluk and Ottoman motifs in a very similar way, with one important difference: as in the sabils in Istanbul at the time, its main façade is rounded.

Top:
Never-ending play of shadows and light on the façade of the sabil–kuttab of 'Abd al-Rahman Katkhuda enhances the intricate design of recessed arches and skillful carving of the columns and *muqarnases*.

This innovation had been introduced to Cairo by Mustafa III's cousin Sultan Mahmud I when he ordered the construction of a sabil–kuttab attached to a convent for the Mawlawiya Sufi order on the bank of the Khalig al-Misri canal, not far from the mosque of Sayida Zeinab. That building, constructed in 1750, nine years before Sultan Mustafa III's sabil, also ingeniously combines Otto-man and Mamluk motifs on its rounded façade. Sultan Mahmud I entrusted the construction of the complex to his kizlar agha, or chief of the black eunuchs in the imperial harem. Thirty-two years earlier, before he was appointed to his post in Istanbul, the same man, named Bashir Agha, had built a sabil–kuttab attached to his own house close from where Sultan Mahmud's would be constructed. The two buildings still stand opposite each other, providing a fine example of how architecture in Cairo evolved within one man's lifetime from traditional forms derived from Mamluk legacy into a style that mixed local and Ottoman motifs.

Opposite page:
The sabil–kuttabs of Sultan Mahmud I (center) and Bashir Agha (right), drawn by Pascal Coste in the 1830s.
Above:
The sabil–kuttab of Sultan Mahmud I in 2009.

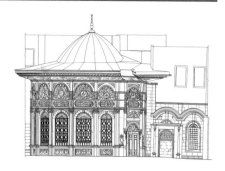

Although sabil–kuttabs of rectangular plan and in the conservative style continued to be built in Cairo, many patrons followed the new trend: seven bow-fronted sabil–kuttabs still survive in the city from the second half of the 18th century, and there were certainly more. The two founded by the Ottoman sultans are closer to Istanbul in their extensive use of marble, while the decorations of the others are carved in the structural masonry of local limestone. All are a compromise between trends fashionable in the imperial capital and the local tradition of Mamluk origin. It would be sixty more years after the construction of Sultan Mustafa III's building before finally, after the shattering political events of the Napoleonic invasion and its aftermath, Muhammad 'Ali Pasha radically disposed of the Mamluk architectural legacy and began to erect buildings in purely Ottoman style in Cairo, starting with the sabil dedicated to his prematurely deceased son Tusun Pasha in 1820. This building owes nothing to the local Cairene tradition. Clad entirely in magnificently carved white marble, it also features a bowed façade, but has no upper floor housing the kuttab and is instead surmounted by a dome like its counterparts in Istanbul. Unadulterated Ottoman architecture continued in Cairo under the rule of Muhammad 'Ali and his descendants, but in the long run it was the Mamluk legacy that prevailed: when Egypt embarked on a search for national identity in the second half of the 19th century, both the royal family and the public at large turned to neo-Mamluk forms to express it.

Above:
The rounded façade of the sabil of Muhammad 'Ali Pasha, 1820.

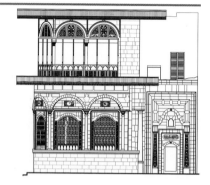

In 1759, Sultan Mustafa apparently found nothing wrong in the local flavoring to his political statement in architectural form. But the bowed façade of his sabil is purely Ottoman in style, even though it is surmounted in Cairene fashion with a kuttab. The three huge windows of the sabil are in shallow recesses under round arches that seem to be supported on very slender engaged columns of marble, while in reality they rest on massive pillars that form the front façade. This can be seen from the inside, but from the outside, the sabil displays a delicate and vivid graphic pattern of arches and marble frames and panels. The windows are topped with segmental arches whose line is enlivened by the s-shape curves of the impost blocks to the sides, producing a very Baroque effect indeed. The marble frames of the windows are carved in gracious floral motifs borrowed from the Rococo architecture fashionable in Europe at the time, but given Ottoman flavor by the use of naturalistically depicted flowers. The bronze window grilles are extremely elaborate; like all sabil grilles, they feature larger openings at the bottom, through which cups of drinking water (chained to the grilles) were passed to the people outside. The façade is built in alternating courses of black, yellowish brown, and white marble, enlivening the building with color in a manner rarely seen in Cairo.

The portal to the right of the sabil, through which one enters the staircase leading to the kuttab, similarly exploits curvilinear forms, contrasting color of different stones, and fine carving in marble. As in the façade of the sabil itself, the overall effect of richness, liveliness, and splendor is achieved by the judicious shaping and combining of different architectural elements, rather than by opulence of ornamentation.

The loggia of the kuttab on the upper story features huge grilles of gypsum paste and stained glass in its arches. The oldest surviving examples of such grilles in Cairo are as ancient as the 9th century, and they were subsequently used in countless Mamluk and Ottoman-period buildings in the city. In the Sabil of Mustafa III, however, their fluid, coiling patterns give the grilles a distinctly Baroque feel seldom found elsewhere in Cairo. There are no wooden brackets under the wide overhanging eaves (as there would be in Mamluk-inspired sabil–kuttabs), but the delicate lace-like wooden fringes are a typically Cairene feature.

Page 95:
The rounded façade of the sabil of Sultan Musafa III introduced pure Ottoman Baroque style to Cairo.
Opposite page:
The kuttab on the upper floor of the building.
Above:
The portal leading to the kuttab.

The most purely Ottoman elements of the façade are found in oval medallions on the marble panels placed above the windows. The calligraphic device in each of them is the tughra–a stylized signature of the Ottoman sultan. In this sign, designed by the court calligrapher for each sultan, every stroke not only is a letter of the alphabet, but also has its own name and its symbolic significance. The three verticals represent flag posts signifying independence; the wavy lines form standards on these posts; the slanting lines to the right represent the sword symbolizing power; the loops to the left signify the outer (around the Mediterranean) and inner (around the Black Sea) realms of the Ottoman Empire. The tughra on this sabil reads: "Mustafa Khan Son of Ahmed, Victorious Forever."

After entering the small but lively alley along the side façade of the sabil–kuttab, one is instantly transported from Istanbul to traditional Cairo. The façade of local limestone has its decoration carved in structural masonry, just like Mamluk-period buildings, and its forms are in the traditional, Mamluk-inspired style. Through the handsome portal in this façade one passes through a small vestibule into a room with a painted and carved ceiling under which runs a frieze of calligraphic panels and with a marble mosaic floor. The room gives access to the service area where water was fetched from the cistern, which is a lofty chamber covered with four domes resting on arches supported on a massive central column. Water

Opposite page:
Tughra of Sultan Mustafa III carved in marble on the sabil's facade.
Above:
Side entrance to the sabil, showing features inspired by Mamluk architecture.

would then be put into a tank from which it flowed into marble basins by the sabil windows to be offered to people.

The sabil itself is also entered from the same room. It has a spacious and richly decorated interior. The ceiling is sumptuously painted in carpet-like floral patterns and partially gilded. A band of calligraphic panels with praises for the sultan in elegantly elongated flowing script runs around the walls on a frieze below the ceiling. Another painted frieze runs halfway up the walls; below it, the walls are lined with marble panels framed with intricate geometric patterns of multicolor marble mosaic. More marble mosaic decorates the floor. The elaborate woodwork of doors, shutters, and built-in wall shelves is handsomely painted. All this decoration successfully blends geometric designs of local Mamluk provenance with floral motifs and color schemes borrowed from Istanbul. But the most striking and most unusual feature of the interior belongs neither on the Nile nor on the Bosphorus, but on the River Amstel: the upper parts of the walls are covered with more than two thousand blue-and-white Dutch wall-tiles.

Opposite page:
The decorated ceiling of the sabil.
Above:
The interior of the sabil after conservation.

AMSTERDAM

IN AMSTERDAM
THE TILES

The Delft Blue

The beer-brewing industry of Delft, a city in southern Holland, went through hard times in the mid-17th century. When a disastrous explosion of the Delft gunpowder magazine on 12 October 1654 devastated much of the city, many of the breweries that were damaged in the catastrophe never recovered. A number of them were bought by master potters, though some workshops retained the old breweries' names after being converted into pottery factories. The transition in Delft from a consumable commodity to a more lasting product in the 17th and 18th centuries had far-reaching consequences. Wall tiles produced in Delft workshops and in similar ones elsewhere in Holland adorn buildings in Portugal, Spain, the Azores, Brazil, France, Germany, Poland, Russia, Estonia, Latvia, Denmark, Sweden, Indonesia, Rajasthan in India, and Sri Lanka. They were present in the houses of New Amsterdam, and continued to be used there and in other areas of what later became the United States for some time after the city was renamed New York. They also found their way to Istanbul and Cairo. So great was the demand that the estimated number of Dutch wall tiles produced in two hundred years was an astonishing eight hundred million.

Delft after the 1654 gunpowder explosion as shown in
a painting by Egbert van der Poel (detail of the painting from
1733 in the Rijksmuseum in Amsterdam).

The potters of Delft were eager to buy old breweries because they needed large premises for their work. Production of wall-tiles and pottery vessels in 17th-century Holland, although definitely pre-industrial, amounted to large operations. A picture of a Delft-type pottery workshop from 1737 is now at the Rijksmuseum in Amsterdam. Previously it was displayed in the Frisian city of Makkum, where a factory making "Delft blue" pottery founded in 1594 still operates, one of only two remaining. The picture shows twenty-six people working simultaneously on different tasks under the direction of the workshop owner and his wife (apparently a very commanding woman), while two horses power turnstiles to operate elaborate machinery. The centerpiece of the workshop is, naturally, the kiln that stretches through all three stories of the huge building. (Appropriately, the picture is painted on a panel of wall-tiles.) In 1668 Delft had twenty-seven pottery workshops that operated forty-two kilns. Of those twenty-seven, eight produced "Delft blue" wall tiles.

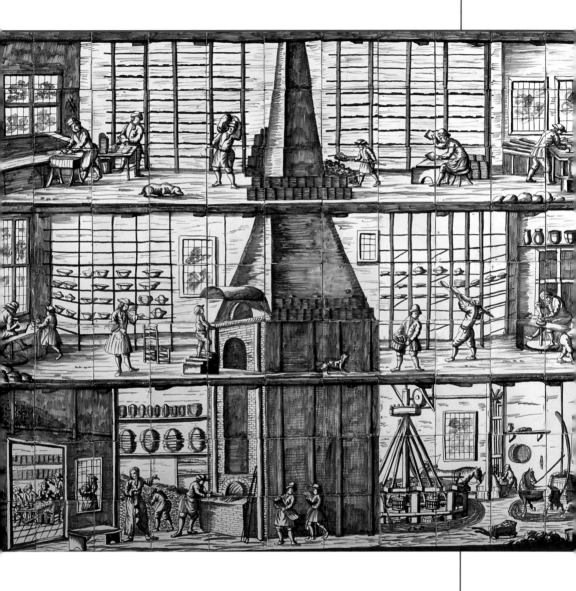

Opposite page and above:
Details of a panel with a depiction of a pottery workshop, 1737
now in the Rijksmuseum in Amsterdam

The type of ceramics produced by such workshops had a long history. Around 800, the Abbasid caliph Harun al-Rashid of Baghdad, who captured the imaginations of both the east and the west by appearing in the *Thousand and One Nights* tales, received a huge gift of luxurious Chinese pottery vessels, including some very early porcelain produced during the T'ang Dynasty. Many such vessels were also excavated from his son and successor's palace in Samara in present-day Iraq. It appears that this marked a point when ceramic vessels began to be seen in the Islamic world not merely as utilitarian objects but also as luxury items and as an artistic medium. Potters in Islamic countries were soon producing outstanding pieces of great variety and fine quality, not just imitations of Chinese products.

They could not replicate the hard, white, and slightly translucent body of Chinese porcelain, however, because they didn't have the kaolin clay from which porcelain is made. To imitate the look of china vessels, the potters of Iraq reinvented tin-glazing, a technique that had been used with the same local materials in ancient Mesopotamia, but was long since forgotten. Tin glaze (also called tin enamel) applied to a vessel after its first firing produces an opaque white vitreous coat on the body of pottery when it is fired once more. If it is painted with suitable pigments before being returned to the kiln, the colors melt into the glaze and are fixed in all their brilliancy during the second firing. This is a different technique from that used later by the Ottoman potters of Iznik, where equally brilliant colors painted on a white pottery body were covered with a transparent lead glaze.

Opposite page:
A bowl produced in the 9th century in Iraq.
Above:
A wall tile from Moorish Spain, 14th or early 15th century.

Both the technique of tin glazing and the associated repertoire of decorative motifs soon spread throughout the Islamic world, including Moorish Spain. From there, and from Arab Sicily, tin glazing reached Europe. In Italy this type of pottery was called maiolica, and maiolica work–plates, vessels, figurines, and architectural ornaments–became an important part of Italian renaissance art. It was from the Italian town of Faenza that the French tin-glazed pottery derived the term faience. Different variants were produced all over Europe, and tin-glazed vessels were being made in Spanish-conquered Mexico by 1540. The Dutch variety is sometimes referred to as "Delft porcelain." This is doubly confusing: although Delft was the main center of production, the so-called delftware was also made in many other cities in the Netherlands; moreover, it is not porcelain, but tin-glazed earthenware. Real porcelain was not made in Europe until sometime around 1707. In its broad sense "Delft" is used for any cobalt blue-on-white or manganese purple-on-white ceramics produced in Holland from the early 17th century on.

Opposite page:
14th-century Italian maiolica bowl, probably from Umbria.
Above:
Maiolica plate from Castel Durante in Italy, ca 1550–70.

In spite of their name, the "Delft blue" tiles were produced throughout Holland. Workshops in Gouda, Amsterdam, Rotterdam, Utrecht, Dordrecht, and Makkum all produced delftware. The Dutch scholar Hans Theunissen, who studied the wall tiles in the sabil of Mustafa III in Cairo, concluded that they were made in Amsterdam.

Tin-glazed pottery was first produced in the Low Countries in the early 16th century by Italian potters in the thriving and cosmopolitan city of Antwerp. They produced tiles that resembled Italian maiolica in their use of different bright colors, but with geometric ornamental patterns surprisingly reminiscent of the Middle Eastern and Islamic origins of tin-glazing and its transfer to northern Europe via Moorish Spain. When the territories of present-day Belgium were taken by the Spanish in 1585, many potters left for the northern Netherlands. There they gradually developed a distinct local style of wall tiles. The individual tiles no longer combined to form continuous geometric patterns; each piece was decorated with a flower or fruit, an animal, people, scenes of everyday life, or Biblical subjects, usually enclosed within a square or a circle, with stylized floral motifs in the corners of the tile. Soon after 1620, Dutch pottery acquired the color scheme in which most of the millions of the "Delft" tiles were painted, and which is still its hallmark feature for most people around the world: cobalt blue on white background. Like the re-invention of tin-glazing in Iraq eight hundred years earlier, the emergence of "Delft blue" resulted from exposure to imported Chinese products.

Opposite page:
18th-century Dutch tiles from the sabil of Sultan Mustafa III in Cairo.
Above:
The blue-on-white color scheme was popular in many centers of production. This modern piece from Lisbon reproduces 17th-century Portugese ceramics.
Right:
A Chinese Ming Dynasty plate.

In 1602 and 1604, two loads of Chinese porcelain carried on Portuguese ships were captured by the Dutch and put on sale by auction, resulting in a fashion for chinaware in Europe. This coincided with the founding of the Dutch East India Company in 1602. Its merchant ships (of which the Company had 150 by 1669, in addition to its 40 ships of war and 10,000 soldiers) soon brought enormous quantities of Chinese porcelain to the Netherlands, fueling demand for local imitations that were more affordable. The imported china at that time was late Ming Dynasty ware, usually decorated in cobalt blue underglaze patterns painted on the white body of the vessels. When the political turmoil in China that followed the death of the Emperor Wanli in 1620—and that also marked the beginning of the end of the Ming dynasty—disrupted imports, this color scheme became dominant in the local production in Holland. To make their wares appear like Ming porcelain, the Dutch potters covered their tin-glazed vessels and tiles with an additional coat of transparent lead glaze.

Through trial-and-error, every detail of the complex process of "Delft blue" pottery production was developed to perfection. The clay used for the pottery body was a mix of three different natural clays: one local, another from the region of Tournai in Flanders, the third from the Ruhr region in Germany. It was prepared for use by washing away impurities, sieving, and drying the thin suspension of fine clay in water into thick paste. This was done in specialized workshops, not at the potteries, to which the mixed clay was delivered by barges traveling the network of canals that connected and crisscrossed every Dutch city. Other specialized workshops providing materials for the potters were tin-ash kilns and paint-grinding windmills. To produce wall-tiles, the clay delivered from the "earth washeries" was kneaded by earth-mixers with their feet, then rolled into thin tablets from which square tiles were cut with a frame, dried, and fired in a kiln at about 1000°C. Once cooled, the tiles were covered on one side with a tin glaze of creamy consistency and then painted.

A Ming dynasty Chinese porcelain plate.

In the process of mass production, the outlines of the painted decoration were transferred onto the tiles with a stencil. This was a piece of paper on which a drawing was made; the lines were pierced with a needle. The stencil was put onto the tile, and a sponge or a pouch with powdered charcoal pressed gently against it, leaving charcoal marks on the tiles where the stencil was punched. The decorator then painted with a brush, using the charcoal lines as guides. This required much skill and a sure hand because as paint was applied to the wet surface of the glaze, no erasures were possible.

The result of such a technique can be observed on the landscape tiles in the sabil of Mustafa III in Cairo. The first impression is one of an almost infinite variety of different scenes. On closer inspection, one notices that in fact many tiles repeat the same composition. Even so, no two tiles are completely identical, because each one was individually painted freehand over the stencil-transferred guidelines. Once painted, the tiles were put in the kiln again and fired for the second time at about the same temperature. Finally, they were covered with a thin coat of transparent lead glaze.

Opposite page:
Tiles in the sabil of Sultan Mustafa III.
Above:
Similar but not identical pairs of tiles from the sabil.

In the highly organized structure of the potter's workshop, with its strict division of labor, the company's shop that sold the final products was typically run by the women of the potter's household, under the direction of the master's wife.

To conduct their business legally, all craftsmen in a city had to belong to a guild that regulated their trade and protected their professional interests. Because they produced painted tiles and vessels, potters were required to be members of the Guild of St. Luke. Since all painters, regardless of their medium, belonged to this guild, the Delft potters rubbed shoulders at its meetings with such professional colleagues as Johannes Vermeer and Pieter de Hooch, while those working in Amsterdam would meet Rembrandt and van Ruisdael. The era that art historians call the golden age of Dutch painting was also the golden age for Dutch pottery.

Opposite page:
Women played their part in the production of Dutch tiles (detail of the painting from 1733
in the Rijksmuseum in Amsterdam).
Above:
The view of Delft by Johannes Vermeer, ca 1660, now at the Royal Arts Gallery Mauritshuis
in The Hague.

Little Holland
on a Different Canal

Two types of tiles appear on the walls of Mustafa III's sabil. One is decorated with small branches, each with two hyacinth flowers, that form a lively pattern with their curving stems and leaves. The flower motifs are placed in the middle of empty white tiles, with no corner motifs, so when put together on a wall, the tiles create an elegant impression of a pure white, glistening wall dotted with small flowers. Most tiles of this type were decorated using the same stenciled pattern; a small number have a similar pattern but with roses instead of hyacinths.

The second type has a circle inscribed within its square shape, with simplified floral motifs in the corners and a landscape scene inside the circle. On these tiles, a panorama of Dutch landscapes and scenes of daily life in Holland unfolds on the walls of the sabil. Cities, villages, bell towers, gates, castles, bridges, houses, and windmills sit in the landscapes filled with trees, lakes, ponds and canals, fields and meadows; distant ships sail the sea and birds fly among the clouds while people go about their business. Tiny figures of men and women work in the fields, ride on horses, hunt with dogs, fish, row boats, travel in carts and coaches, milk or herd their farm animals, engage in conversations and even flirt; they exchange greetings, eat and drink, or just rest in the shadow.

Blue-and-white Dutch tiles from the sabil of Sultan Mustafa III in Cairo.

This display of figurative painting is quite surprising in a building intended to house an Islamic religious charity, but people who received water from the sabil would not normally enter the room. Looking inside through the bronze window grilles, they would not see the details of the paintings, but rather a pattern of blue and white panels: very appropriate colors for a place distributing water. Cobalt blue on white was the predominant color combination on the Turkish tiles produced in Kütahia in the first half of the 18th century, so the decorators of the sabil were probably familiar with this simple color scheme. They were clearly more interested in the overall color of the tiles than in the individual pictures. Because the floral tiles look predominantly white, and the landscape ones give the impression of blue with touches of white, Sultan Musta-fa's builders used them to form decorative bands and panels of contrasting color. Where complete tiles did not fit into a panel, the builders unceremoniously cut away parts of the landscape decoration.

How did twenty-five hundred painted tiles produced by the side of one of the canals of Amsterdam end up on the bank of Khalig al-Misri canal in Cairo? To answer the question, Hans Theunissen had to turn himself temporarily from scholar to detective. In his 2006 article in the *Electronic Journal of Oriental Studies* of Utrecht University he could only present circumstantial evidence rather than irrefutable proofs, but the investigation itself was fascinating enough. The testimony is as follows.

Opposite page:
A Turkish vessel from Kütahia in the collection of Muhammad Mahmud Khalil Museum in Cairo.
Above:
Interior of the sabil of Sultan Mustafa III.

By the second half of the 18th century, good-quality, locally produced wall tiles were no longer available in Istanbul. The reasons for this are not entirely clear, but the fact remains that from the middle of the century the workshops of Kütahia, which took over the production of pottery from the Iznik kilns, increasingly made polychrome pottery vessels. Apparently, blue and white wall tiles that followed Chinese and Dutch examples, and that had once been so popular, were going out of fashion at the time. A sultan who wanted to use wall tiles in a building had to resort to buying them abroad (or to recycling earlier ones). This may have been partly due to a change of taste: it appears that the rich and powerful in 18th-century Istanbul, including the sultan, preferred high-quality imported wares over local products.

In October 1756, a year before the accession of Mustafa III to the throne and three years before the completion of his sabil–kuttab in Cairo, Mustafa's predecessor Sultan Osman III ordered the Ottoman authorities in Belgrade to send twelve crates of ceramic tiles to Istanbul as soon as they arrived from Vienna. The tiles, according to this document, were intended for decoration of imperial buildings and had been purchased on behalf of the court by an English merchant from Galata, where most foreign traders in Istanbul resided. Although the document hints that these were "Viennese tiles," it seems likely that they were in fact Dutch, possibly bought by the Englishman in Germany or Austria, where many Dutch tiles were brought for local use or to be sent to Poland or Russia.

Opposite page and above:
Turkish vessels from Kütahia in the collection of the Muhammad Mahmud Khalil Museum in Cairo.

There is a good chance that these were the same tiles that eventually ended up in Cairo. At any rate, it seems certain that the tiles in Mustafa III's sabil came to Egypt via Istanbul, not directly from Europe. In the Topkapi palace, a passage between the Imperial Hall and the adjacent pantry was lined in the 18th century, almost certainly during Osman III's reign, with Dutch tiles decorated with the "small flower" motif. The tiles there are identical to the rose-decorated ones of which several specimens can be seen on the walls in the sabil of Mustafa III. This logically explains why so few were used in Cairo: the majority were taken out of the lot and stayed in Istanbul, installed in Topkapisaray.

Why did Sultan Osman decide to use only some of the tiles in Istanbul? Perhaps being ferociously religious, he did not want figural representations in the palace. The purchase was made through an intermediary, possibly many intermediaries, and the sultan and his officials may have been surprised when they opened the crates from Belgrade. Or perhaps, being near the end of his reign and his life, he just did not have the time or interest to decide what to do with the tiles. Yet another possibility is that the tiles were primarily intended from the beginning to be used in Cairo, where the Mamluk beys evidently needed to be reminded of the sultan's authority. However it may have been, it appears that when he came to the throne, Mustafa III inherited from his predecessor a set of "Delft blue" wall tiles and possibly with them the idea that they should be used in Cairo. Some pieces of the architectural decoration of the sabil appear to have been prefabricated in Istanbul and shipped to Egypt. It is quite probable that the tiles were sent along with them. If the Mamluk dignitary Abd al-Rahman Katkhuda had built in Cairo his magnificent sabil–kuttab with the intention of outdoing the Ottoman governor by lining its interior with wall tiles, then here was an excellent opportunity to show that the Ottoman sultan could better him with the most fashionable and most luxurious imported ware.

Interior of the sabil of Sultan Mustafa III In Cairo.

Could the tiles in Cairo have been an altogether different set than the ones sent from Vienna via Belgrade to Osman III? That is also possible. We are unlikely ever to know for sure. For the people busy with their everyday activities among the Dutch landscapes on the painted tiles in the sabil, this does not seem to matter at all. They seem as happy and relaxed as they were 250 years ago, when an extraordinary convergence of different cultures, histories, and ideas took them from the canal banks of the Netherlands and put them on the bank of a canal in Cairo.

Opposie and above:
Wall tiles in the sabil of Sultan Mustafa III in Cairo.

THE TALE
OF A MUTE STORYTELLER

THE TALE
OF A MUTE STORYTELLER

The Story
of Ninety Thousand Days

■

Pious deed of the sultan, son of the sultan, Sultan Mustafa Khan. May God perpetuate his reign. [Built in the] year 1173.

This Arabic inscription has adorned the façade of the sabil–kuttab of Mustafa III since it was erected 250 years ago. What does it take to have a building erected? It requires a will and a decision of the founder, the choice of location, and the securing of funds for the construction. Then, the indication of a desired style or drafting a design is just a beginning of a long process. At what point during construction, as craftsmen put together stones, bricks and mortar, does the building become an entity that possesses its own voice? Buildings can speak through words carved on a façade, but also in many other ways. If its stones could talk, what stories would the building created as the pious deed of Sultan Mustafa III tell?

The underground cistern was certainly built first. Not only is it physically the foundation of the building, it is also the essence of the sabil's purpose, the place where water for the pious offering was stored. Hidden from view, the cistern with its single massive pillar supporting the covering arches and domes is the heart of the building. On its plastered walls, many lines indicate various levels of water that was stored there during the last 250 years. How many mugs of water were drawn from this cistern to quench the thirst of so many people before it ceased to be used?

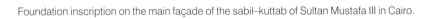
Foundation inscription on the main façade of the sabil–kuttab of Sultan Mustafa III in Cairo.

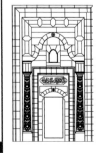

If we are willing to listen, the building can tell us clearly about many things. It speaks about the politics in the 18th century; about the ambitions and the tastes of its founder and of the public in Cairo; about the materials and techniques that its builders used. It speaks about air pollution and a rising groundwater table in 20th- and 21st-century Cairo; about previous conservation efforts; even about clever tricks that Dutch decorators learned to perform with their brushes to bring variety to mass-produced wall tiles. And still, there are so many unanswered questions that would all be solved if only these stones and bricks could talk aloud.

We know that the blue-and white Dutch tiles came from the Netherlands to adorn the building in Cairo, almost certainly traveling via Istanbul. But what about the marble pieces? Were they prepared by stonecutters in Istanbul and shipped over the Mediterranean Sea? Or did Turkish craftsmen come to Cairo to work on the façade? Who was the architect or master builder? Did he follow design drawings, and if so what did they look like? Did the stonecutters carve decorative motifs before mounting them on the façade, as was the usual practice in Europe? Or did they assemble the marble lining on the façade first, and then carve it, following the Cairene building tradition? This is how local builders still work today. It is not unusual to find signatures or marks left discreetly by stonecutters on buildings, but the sabil–kuttab of Sultan Mustafa III keeps its secrets well—no signature was left there.

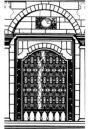

Opposite page:
Dutch tiles in the sabil.
Above:
Detail of the marble carving on the main façade.

Where were the elaborate bronze grilles of the sabil's windows cast? The metal conservator who compared the grilles with those in the sabil of Lady Nafisa al-Bayda, which was built in 1796, concluded that they were technologically extremely similar. Is it possible that they were all shipped from Istanbul? This is highly unlikely in the case of Lady Nafisa's building. Does that mean that Sultan Mustafa's architect, who perhaps had marble pieces for the sabil's façade prefabricated in Istanbul, had enough confidence in Cairo's foundries for the grilles to be manufactured locally?

How did artists decorate the interior of the sabil? Did the local craftsmen who laid the marble floors and executed the dado decoration on the walls in the geometrical Mamluk tradition work hand in hand with Turkish painters who painted Ottoman-style flowers on the ceiling? Or were these flowers painted by local artists who adopted the style? Who decided what poems were to be written on the friezes? Who wrote them? Who was the calligrapher? We know that the erection of the building took two years, but even after the construction dust settled, the story told by the building continued to be riddled with unanswered questions. Who was its first keeper and who was the first servant to offer water to the thirsty ones?

Opposite page:
Detail of the front façade.
Above:
Interior of the sabil.

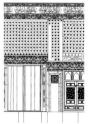

Offering water and keeping a school in a sabil–kuttab were not only pious deeds and a way to perpetuate one's memory, but also a public service. These charities were kept functioning by religious endowments. A foundation charter for such an endowment or *waqf* established in minute detail the revenues assigned to the charity and how they were to be expended. However, Sultan Mustafa III's sabil–kuttab waqf charter could not be located in the archives in Cairo, and it was presumed that the document was lost. Then, in a 'stop press' development, the Turkish scholar Filiz Yenişehirlioğlu of Başkent University in Ankara discovered the document in the archive of the General Directorate of Waqfs in Ankara while she was doing research for this book. It endowed the sabil–kuttab with the revenue from the Sultan's shares in two villages in Giza and prescribed how it was to be distributed. Ten students of the kuttab received stipends (a yearly payment and a monthly amount of pocket-money); in return they were obliged say certain prayers for the sultan and his family at set times. The payroll included

Groupe des sakas au bord du Nil.

Opposite page:
An 18th-century sabil–kuttab, depicted still in use in the late 19th century.
Above:
Water carriers in Cairo captured on an old postcard.

one servant, another person who was responsible for prayers, two "properly dressed" men to carry water to the sabil, a keeper of the lamps (in Ramadan, sabils operated at night), a man in charge of the maintenance of water conduits, and two book-keepers. Yearly sums were assigned for the maintenance of the sabil, for the cleaning of the cistern, for oil and wicks for the lamps, for tuition of the ten students, for their clothing, and for the floor-mats on which they sat in the kuttab. As was the custom, the foundation also distributed money to the poor of Mecca and Medina.

For many generations the building served the people of the neighborhood by offering drinking water to the thirsty and education to the children. E. W. Lane described the functioning of a sabil some seventy years after Sultan Mustafa founded his sabil–kuttab:

Many of the Sebee'ls are remarkable buildings. The general style of a large sabee'l may be thus described.—The principal part of the front is of semicircular form, with three windows of brass grating. Within each window is a trough of water, and when any one would drink, he puts his hand through one of the lowest apertures of the grating, and dips in the trough the brass mug, which is chained to one of the bars.

Opposite page:
Water bottle seller as depicted on an old postcard.
Above:
The openings in the bronze window grilles in the sabil of Sultan
Mustafa III from which mugs of drinking water were offered.

It is easy to imagine people stopping at the sabil for a mouthful of fresh water from the marble basins behind the ornate bronze grilles and having a glimpse of the glossy tiles, polished marble panels, and colorful paintings inside. Above the sabil, in the arcaded loggia of the kuttab, daily instructions were given to the pupils. Again, Lane's description can help us imagine the activities there:

The school-master and his pupils sit upon the ground, and each boy has his tablet in his hands, or a copy of the Kur-an, or of one of its thirty sections, and a little kind of desk of palm-sticks. All the boys in learning to read, recite or chant their lessons aloud, at the same time rocking their heads and bodies incessantly backwards and forwards; which practice is observed by almost all persons in reciting Kur-an; being thought to assist memory. The noise may be imagined. [In a footnote, Lane added: The usual punishment is beating on the soles of the feet with a palm stick.]

Did the perceptive Englishman describe what he saw first-hand at the sabil–kuttab of Mustafa III? He certainly knew the area well, because during one of his stays in Cairo he rented a house very close to the building; his landlady's name, incidentally, translates to "Bed of Tulips."

Opposite page:
A student in a kuttab depicted by E.W. Lane in the 1830s.
Above:
The Holy Qur'an recited in the sabil in 2009.

For decades after decades, the sabil–kuttab of Sultan Mustafa III silently witnessed the vivid daily life of its neighborhood and the Khalig al-Misri canal, the neighboring lakes filling with water during the inundation and turning into gardens as the water receded, and the continuing veneration of Sayida Zeinab's shrine and the annual festivals there. How many generations of people were aware of the political message of power that Sultan Mustafa III wanted to convey when he decided to erect this building? How long did the neighborhood associate his name with the Sublime Porte, and not just with a building that became a fixture in the Sayida Zeinab district?

At the time when the sabil–kuttab of Sultan Mustafa III was erected, the city of Cairo was prosperous, and so it was described by the early 19th-century chronicler al-Gabarti: "Egypt of this period was a dazzling beauty. At that time, wellbeing spread throughout the city, security reigned, prosperity has taken root." One measure of the prosperity was the buildings that sprang up across the city. Among them, the charitable sabil–kuttabs were numerous. The surveyors of the *Description de l'Égypte* counted around 300 of them dispensing drinking water and knowledge in Cairo in 1798.

Mustafa III's building continued to be a silent witness to the fate of its neighborhood when things turned for the worse during the 1770s. The economy faltered as a result of commercial competition from the European countries. The 1780s saw economic crises, poor harvests, rising prices, outbreaks of epidemics, and famine. Al-Gabarti wrote: *Men, women, and children gathered in the streets and markets, shouting out, crying with misery all day and all night long. . . . In the streets you could not take a step without treading on human creatures overcome with poverty and hunger. People fought over the flesh of corpses, donkeys and horses. There were even people who ate little children.*

For centuries, sabil–kuttabs have been the hallmarks of the cityscapes of Cairo. This one in the Bayn al-Qasrayn area was repicted by the Scottish artist David Roberts in 1838.

Then the sabil–kuttab witnessed the French invasion. In early July 1798 a French expeditionary force of some 365 ships carrying 54,000 men, 1,250 horses, and 170 field guns arrived off Alexandria, causing panic there and in Cairo. Napoleon Bonaparte, at the head of the expedition, tried to convince the Egyptians that he came to relieve them of their oppressors and that he and his soldiers were good Muslims. Soon, however, he had to face popular resistance in addition to the harassing Mamluk and Ottoman troops, and Admiral Horatio Nelson's fleet. He left to seek glory in Paris, and in 1801 the French withdrew from Egypt.

A local tale told in the Sayida Zeinab neighborhood relates that at one point Napoleon had his headquarters in the sabil–kuttab of Sultan Mustafa III. There is no historical record to confirm this, but it is fascinating to see how distant historical events are still present in popular imagination after more than two hundred years. The origin of the story can probably be explained by the fact that many of the scholars who accompanied the French expedition and collected material later compiled in the *Description de l'Égypte* were stationed in the neighborhood, in the house that the French requisitioned from Ibrahim Katkhuda al-Sinnari. The recently renovated house stands close to the sabil–kuttab of Mustafa III in an alley called Monge Street, after Gaspard Monge, a member of the expedition who is remembered as the father of differential geometry. Ibrahim al-Sinnari, it might be noted, was also quite distinguished though in a different way: he made his fortune exploiting his skills in occult pursuits.

Opposite page:
The memory of the Napoleonic expedition lives on in street names and in popular tradition.
Above:
Jean-Léon Gérôme's portrait of Napoleon in Cairo, ca 1867–68.

Publication of the *Description de l'Égypte* took twenty years, and the mammoth book was never easily accessible; but it was nevertheless instrumental in arousing interest in the history, society, and natural history of Egypt. In this way, it can be seen as indirectly contributing to the creation of the Comité de Conservation des Monuments de l'Art Arabe established within the Ministry of Awqaf (or Pious Foundations) in December 1881. The Comité effectively saved the Islamic architectural heritage of Cairo for us to see today. Virtually all buildings listed as historic monuments in the city were at some point conserved by the Comité, which also monitored and recorded the buildings, as well as the conservation work done on them. These records, published in French and Arabic in the Comité's *Bulletins*, are invaluable today for anyone involved in conservation of Cairene historic architecture or in related historical research. The handsome volumes, usually bound in brown leather with gold lettering, can be found on the shelves of all respectable research libraries in Cairo; nowadays, they can also be accessed online.

Thanks to these volumes we were able to learn a lot about the fate of the sabil–kuttab of Sultan Mustafa III in the 19th and 20th centuries. More information can be found in the archives of the Supreme Council of Antiquities' Islamic and Coptic Sector, into which the Comité de Conservation des Monuments de l'Art Arabe was transformed in 1952, and which is the custodian of Cairo's architectural heritage today. In these archives, located in the Citadel of Cairo, one can find yellowed documents and photographs that tell the story of various historic buildings in Cairo, among them the sabil–kuttab of Sultan Mustafa III.

Opposite page:
Publications of the Comité are a precious source of information about Cairo's monuments.
Above:
The sabil–kuttab of Sultan Mustafa III in a late 19th-century photograph.

The first entry to be found in the Comité's *Bulletin* about the building dates to 1886 and refers to a "magnificent specimen of architecture of the last époque of Arabic style, under the domination of the Turks." It reports that the building was used as a sabil and a kuttab, and mentions its decoration in colorful marble, bronze grilles, and "faiences" in the interior. This means that for a hundred and twenty-five years the building had been continuously used and that its decoration survived, although there were problems with an encroaching wall erected by a neighbour.

In 1889 six copper cups with incised decoration dating to the mid-18th century were transferred from the sabil–kuttab of Sultan Mustafa III to the Museum of Islamic Art, at that time located within the partially ruined mosque of al-Hakim; the present building on Port Said Street was only built in 1902, after the Khalig al-Misri canal was filled in. Contemporary mugs were purchased and attached with chains to the bronze grilles, so even in the late nineteenth century the sabil was still being used as it was intended when it was constructed. Also in 1889 the first repairs to the blue-and-white tiles in the sabil were made, although the *Bulletin* does not mention that the tiles were Dutch. And serious maintenance problems were

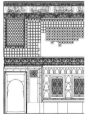

Opposite page and above:
Details of the sabil's interior after conservation in 2009.

also recorded that year when the Comité's delegation reported refuse "of unsatisfactory cleanliness" dumped in the sabil by the sheikh of the kuttab, as well as garbage from the neighboring mosque of Sayida Zeinab.

The Comité conducted repairs in 1891. These were replacement of disintegrated stone blocks in the entrance portal to the kuttab and repairs to the pavement of the sabil and the adjacent rooms. The cost, covered from the "reserve for small works," was 55 Egyptian Pounds—an amount that would not carry us very far in 2009. Two years later sanitary services attempted to disinfect the kuttab against a contagious disease by covering it with a disinfecting paint that contained "a little arsenic." Fortunately the decorated ceiling was spared overpainting. The *Bulletin* does not mention the nature of the disease, but it was probably the cholera epidemic that swept the Ottoman Empire and beyond in 1893–94.

In 1914, the Comité reported damage to the marble lining of the sabil due to humidity. It was caused by leakage in the plumbing system of the marble basins, which were then dismantled, repaired, and re-installed. This again confirms the continuing use of the sabil. That same year, the faulty marble lining on the pillars between the arched windows in the sabil was replaced with artificial marble, i.e., reinforced cement mortar imitating stone. The pavement in the sabil was repaired as well.

Opposite page:
A brass water mug found in excavations during the conservation of the late 18th-century sabil of Nafisa al-Bayda in Cairo. It was chained to the sabil window grille—a link of the chain is still attached.
Above:
Interior of the kuttab in Mustafa III's building in 2008, before conservation.

The school in the kuttab also remained in use and kept asking for more room for its activities. A request by the schoolmaster in 1909 to construct an additional classroom in the main entrance area was rejected. Another application, this time to use the sabil room as a dining room for students, was also rejected in 1911, but finally approved in July 1917. From this we may infer that the sabil had at last lost its purpose as piped water became available in the vicinity, but it also shows that the building, which now functioned entirely as a school, continued to serve the needs of its neighborhood.

In 1926–27 repairs to the sabil room marble cladding were again necessary after part of it collapsed. The schoolmaster, Omar Lotfy, had a wooden floor installed over the marble pavement at that time because the stone floor was too cold for the students—which also tells us that they still studied sitting in a Turkish manner on the floor. But when the floor was removed in 1934 and the wood used to build partition walls in the sabil, it was reported that the students' benches were damaging the marble floor, so the practice of sitting on the floor had clearly been discontinued. The building began to deteriorate seriously in 1952 when it was reported that the school's upstairs toilet and the cistern below the building were both in very bad condition, causing deterioration to the ceilings and creating a health hazard.

It was also in 1952 that a charitable organization for helping the families of cancer victims was established in the sabil room, and it is still housed in the building. So the building had two independent users, the charity and the school. The following year the Ministry of Health recommended closure of the cistern because it accumulated sewage, but nothing was done, and the recommendation was repeated thirteen years later in 1966. Meanwhile, a similarly unsatisfactory situation persisted with the upstairs toilet as is indicated by reports of serious damage caused by leakage that were filed in 1958, 1961, and 1967.

The sabil–kuttab of Sultan Mustafa III in a photograph from the Supreme Council of Antiquities archive.

This means that even in the late 1960s the kuttab continued to operate as a school. But that function must have lapsed soon afterward. In any case, nothing was found in the archives from the 1970s and 1980s except a memo from 1982 reporting that parts of the wooden decoration of the overhanging eaves *(rafraf)* had collapsed. The Supreme Coucil of Antiquities (SCA) carried out conservation work in 1992–94, while the charity continued to use the sabil. The intervention included the over-painting of the original ceiling decoration and the reattachment of tiles. In 1999 the external facades were hurriedly cleaned for the opening of the new extension to the Sayida Zeinab mosque. Finally, in 2001 another conservation intervention was done by the SCA. This consisted of structural repairs: filling cracks, re-plastering, removal of a faulty floor upstairs, and repairs to the roof. The roof repairs were problematic because they overburdened the structure with heavy layers of sand and mortar. The work was reported to be progressing slowly, and it came to a full stop in 2007. This coincided with the request by the Netherlands-Flemish Institute to carry out its recent conservation project.

The picture that emerges from the historical documents is one of a building that is not only a testimony to the architectural style of the time when it was built, but also a living part of its neighborhood, whose needs it continues to serve.

The sabil–kuttab has faced essentially the same problems and challenges since the late 19th century. Deterioration of the fabrics due to moisture, aging, and wear and tear have not changed. Water has been always the most serious factor of deterioration, whether faulty plumbing of the marble basins of the sabil, inefficient sewage system of the toilets, or accumulated sewage in the cistern. Human-related damage reported in 1889 (refuse dumped in the sabil) was identical to the problems that the recent conservation project encountered every day. The pressures of urban development, first reported in 1886 in the form of encroaching structures, are still present: the buffer zone established around the building in 2003 is used today by local peddlers.

Above:
The sabil–kuttab is inseparable from the life of its neighborhood.
Right:
Water carriers in Cairo on an old postcard.

The bottom line is that there is no point in trying to deny or defy the physical, social, urban, and environmental challenges affecting the building and the neighborhood. The only way to ensure the survival and preservation of a historic building is to secure its sustained and continued proper maintenance after any one-time conservation effort is completed.

Seen in this perspective, the recently completed conservation was not "the end of history" for the sabil–kuttab. It could not solve its problems for all time by fixing it in an optimal and permanent condition. Rather, it is just another chapter in the story that the building has been silently narrating for 250 years. If conservation can enable the monument to stay vocal for many more years to come, that is the most that a conservation architect can hope to achieve. But it is the building alone who decides what it says, not the conservator.

Opposite page:
A glass of refreshing drink can be bought today in Cairo from a street seller no different from the one photographed in the early 20th century.
Above:
Detail of the façade of Sultan Mustafa III's sabil–kuttab after conservation in 2009.

Conservation: The Treatment

■

The conservation project that was carried out in 2008–2009 under the direction of Agnieszka Dobrowolska was financed by the Embassy of the Kingdom of the Netherlands from the Local Cultural Fund and affiliated to the Netherlands-Flemish Institute in Cairo. As is the case with all conservation work in Egypt, it was done in cooperation with and under supervision of the Supreme Council of Antiquities, which is the legal custodian of the monument.

The limestone and marble façades were cleaned and protected, and hollow joints filled with mortar. The wooden overhanging eaves were also repaired by skilled carpenters and cleaned. "Cleaning," it should be understood, is a straightforward word when it applies to housekeeping: any kind of dirt and dust is removed, and the more completely the better. Not so in the conservation of a historic building where over-cleaning can cause irreparable damage. One has to learn what actually covers the façades and interior walls: Is this just dirt? Or is it coatings that were intentionally applied? If they were not applied by the original builders and decorators but by someone else at a later date, should they be retained or removed? Sample-collection, thorough analyses, and test cleanings must precede any serious conservation. This was also the case with the work on the sabil–kuttab of Mustafa III.

Above and right:
Conservators at work on the bronze window grilles of the sabil of Sultan Mustafa III.

Overlying layers of dirt were removed from the bronze grilles in the windows. Then, pockets of corrosion were cleaned out with minute drills, very much in the manner of a dentist's work. Further corrosion was arrested by application of a chemical agent, then the entire surfaces of the grilles were protected by microcrystalline wax, which was applied hot so it could penetrate deeper and fill every microscopic pore in the cast.

The white-and-blue tiles in the sabil's interior were conserved. Out of the 2025 original tiles preserved on the walls, 450 were detached from their supporting base of lime mortar where cavities had formed behind them. In effect, huge portions of the tile panels were held together only by the touching edges of the tiles and could fall off the walls at any moment. Therefore the conservation of the tiles was an emergency intervention. Liquid mortar was injected into the cavities with syringes (again and again, treatment of a weakened building brings medical procedures to mind). In line with the project's overall philosophy of using traditional materials and techniques similar to those of the original construction, the fixing agent consisted of slaked lime and stone powder mixed with water. But wherever it was necessary for structural reasons, modern materials and technologies were used; in this case, an acrylic emulsion was added to ensure firm adhesion of the tiles to the wall. Only after the stabilization were the surfaces of the tiles cleaned and the joints between them re-pointed.

Opposite page, above, and right:
Conservators' work at the sabil–kuttab required not only skills, but also patience and precision.

The ceiling of the sabil, sumptuously decorated with Ottoman Baroque floral patterns, probably presented the conservators with their greatest challenge. A preliminary investigation revealed that the background of the painting was originally light green, typical of the color scheme preferred in Ottoman work of the time. But over time an almost black film had formed over the paint through oxidation. To make matters worse, the ceiling underwent a rather heavy-handed conservation in 1990s when the blackened background was repainted in black oil paint, and not very precisely. Much consideration was required to decide on the extent of intervention. After all, the objectives of the work were to preserve and protect the surviving original materials and to respect all phases of the building's history, not to introduce 21st-century re-creations. The conservators chose to clean and restore an area where the original decoration was best preserved under the over-painting in order to show the original color scheme.

Opposite page, above, and right:
Conservation of painted and gilded woodwork at the sabil.

The woodwork in the sabil room presented another surprise. Its doors and shutters were skilfully constructed from small pieces of wood assembled in tongue-and-groove joinery to form decorative geometric patterns, a technique carried over from medieval Mamluk times; built-in cupboards were shaped with gracious curving arches. All of that had been covered with multiple layers of cheap paint. But when the conservators removed those layers, they were astonished to find Ottoman floral decoration on the woodwork—faded and damaged, but still clearly discernible. As Hans Theunissen wrote in 2006:

> The interior of the sabil of Sultan Mustafa III still largely is as it was 250 years ago. It is a time capsule of mid-18th-century Ottoman interior decoration and for this reason its importance for Ottoman art history can hardly be overestimated.

The subsequent conservation work has proven that the time capsule is even more intact than Theunissen observed.

Opposite page, above, and right:
Wooden cupboards in the sabil during and after conservation in 2009.

Last, but by no means least, the cistern was cleared. Causing hygienic problems since the 1950s because leaked sewage had seeped into it through cracks in the walls, it was a messy task to handle and presented a less inspiring prospect than fine conservation of paintings or marble, but it was not less needed. After the water was pumped out, the residue deposited over 250 years had to be removed. For weeks on end, a small army of men equipped with hoes, rubber baskets, and protective clothing carried away the black, smelly mud from the cistern. (Whether the workers called a hoe a *fas* or a *turya* depended on whether they originally came from Lower or Upper Egypt.) Now the cistern is quite impressive. As these words are being written, a permanent pump has been installed, allowing one to hope that the cistern will soon be made accessible to visitors.

The conservation work resulted in making more space in the building available to the charity that operates in it. The sabil room, however, was adapted for public visitation as a historic interior. A small display explaining the building, its decoration, and its recent conservation was installed inside. Designing the display to be attractive and informative while not competing or interfering with the original decoration was another challenging task.

Opposite page, above, and right:
Cleaning the cistern under the sabil was a challenging task.

Conservation: The People

"Structure was reinforced," "surface was cleaned," "comprehensive documentation was produced," "protective coat was applied"—one reads such phrases again and again in specialist conservation reports. And they are all true, but they sound so impersonal as to convey an impression that professional operations happen by themselves, mechanically, almost without human involvement. Precisely the opposite is true with any architectural conservation project. No two historic buildings are the same; no matter how much careful planning is done, surprises will be encountered and secrets revealed; no matter how precisely analyses are performed, there is never a fixed, universal recipe for optimal treatment. Ultimately, it all depends on the conservators and craftsmen whose skilled and caring hands touch every square inch of the building during the process of conservation. Their skill, experience, judgment, understanding of the monument, and willingness to listen to it allow the building to tell its story.

Egyptian and foreign conservators worked hand in hand in the sabil–kuttab.

They delicately tapped tiles and plaster to locate cavities by ear, for even in the age of sophisticated methods of remote-sensing, this is still the surest way. They removed layers of grime and dust in minute trial openings on painted surfaces to establish the best methods for cleaning and protection. They studied all signs of deterioration to understand its patterns in order to halt it and prevent its reoccurrence. Conservation is an interdisciplinary effort. Fine arts conservators were assisted by surveyors who accurately mapped the building and its deterioration, and by photographers who recorded the condition of the sabil–kuttab before and after conservation. They worked hand in hand with local craftsmen producing replacement pieces and working on the building's masonry and woodwork. Architectural conservation of even a fairly small building means running a construction site, and the skills of the site manager were essential.

Conservation is also about swapping ideas and experiences. First and foremost, it is teamwork, and it is this aspect of working on a conservation site that is perhaps the most satisfying. Could the team working on a building that blends so many different traditions and histories as the sabil–kuttab of Sultan Mustafa III be anything but international and colorful itself?

Experienced veterans and young trainees alike contributed their efforts to the conservation project.

Laurence, a French stone conservator, is renowned in historic Cairo for her fondness for fried liver sandwiches. The Sayida Zeinab area is abundant with various food stands, so she could have her favorite for lunch every day, and always in choice quality. She brought a charming French sound to her Arabic, which otherwise has a distinctly Upper Egyptian accent.

From the appearance of the young Egyptian architect Yasmine, who was the project's site manager and engineer, it would be difficult to guess that this usually soft-spoken, considerate, and gentle-looking person possesses formidable management skills. Her professional experience, including running hundred-strong teams of people, helped make the construction site move like well-oiled machinery while she kept smiling as if it required no effort.

Erico is a German-speaking conservator from South Tyrol in Italy. Sharing his time between Germany and Egypt for more than a decade, he is an embodiment of infinite patience when he spends hours cleaning minute details of painted decoration. Sometimes tests revealed that the best cleaning agent in a particular situation would be saliva; the modern chemical industry has still not been able to synthetically reproduce its enzymatic contents. Erico was always ready to share the secrets of his trade with his Egyptian assistants, who followed his instructions skilfully.

Asma' worked on painted decoration and was extremely adept at recording conservation work on documentation drawings. The prettiest conservator on the project, she felt she needed to wear trousers when working high on scaffolding, but she would never give up her stylish long skirts, always carefully color-coordinated with her head-scarf. Wearing both was not easy in the heat of Cairo summer, but for Asma' there was no compromise when style and fashion were concerned. In spite of being so busy working on the decorated ceilings, she managed to get married during the course of the project.

Reinhold, a metal conservator from Germany, quickly established a cordial working relationship with his assistants, although he does not speak Arabic. Non-verbal communication, and the bond of shared cigarettes and of good professional understanding gave "the boys," as he called his assistants, the necessary training to complete the conservation of bronze grilles, one of the project's most challenging tasks, after he and his wife left for Germany.

Salah the Carpenter (also known as Abu Rami after the name of a son he is particularly proud of) has been working on conservation projects for close to twenty years. In the small family-run workshop that he owns in the traditional Cairo neighborhood of Dar al-Salam, his sons learn the skills and secrets of the trade by working as his assistants; they often helped him in the sabil. When we first met Salah during the conservation of a medieval mosque in the early 1990s, these young men were toddlers, and some perhaps not yet born.

The Southern Cairo Inspectorate of the Islamic and Coptic Sector of the Supreme Council of Antiquities is a very somber-sounding name. In reality, its supervision of the project was not bureaucratic drudgery but a friendly exchange of ideas and experiences—and not a small amount of local gossip—that took place over countless small cups of strong, heavily sweetened tea.

Naser, an experienced conservator in charge of the Egyptian conservation team, always took time to enjoy a chat with his young personnel while sitting on a cushion on the floor over a cup of Turkish coffee, his greying hair not affecting the camaraderie.

Tariq, the youngest of the team, made a point that his blue overalls with the white logo of the project always be immaculately clean. How he managed this when he was efficiently removing 250 years of dust from the sabil's ceiling remains his secret.

These were just a few of the team's participants. Usually some twenty people were busy in the building at any particular time, and altogether about a hundred individuals worked on the project. They were all part of the conservation team, and as they worked in the neighborhood they also belonged to a broader community of the Sayida Zeinab area, which so truthfully embodies the spirit of Cairo, the Mother of the World.

The boats on the Khalig Canal, the donkey carts, and the camels have been replaced with motor vehicles of every possible description, but otherwise things stay the same in Cairo. Merchants display and loudly advertise their wares, which tend to be seasonal. (Many people in Europe and America have forgotten that fruits and vegetables were not always available all year round; they do not know the joy of savoring truly fresh produce.) Shoes and clothes of any imaginable color and design can be bought, and seemingly irreparably ruined garments can be skilfully restored next to the sabil. The best kebab shop in town is just around the corner. True, much of the merchandise on offer nowadays comes from China or Korea, but Cairo has always traded in products from afar. If an Ottoman sultan could bring tiles from Holland to the neighborhood 250 years ago, then have things really changed that much?

How best to finish this story of a building that brings together Cairo, Istanbul, and Amsterdam in unexpected ways, and of the countless people who have interacted with it throughout the past 250 years? Perhaps by just quoting from the Charter of Venice, which was drafted fifty-five years ago to set internationally accepted standards for preservation of historic heritage, and which remains the touchstone for anybody who is involved in architectural conservation:

> *Imbued with a message from the past, the historic monuments of generations of people remain to the present day as living witnesses of their age-old traditions.*

Illustration Credits

Photographs by:
Agnieszka Dobrowolska: 59 (bottom), 61 (top), 67 (bottom), 73 (bottom), 75 (bottom), 93, Chapter 3-margins, 181 (top)
Jan Dobrowolski: 63 (top), 164, 165 (top)
Jaroslaw Dobrowolski: ix (left and center), Chapter 1-margins, 1, 3 (top), 4 (top), 5, 7, 9, 11 (top),15, 19, 21, 22, 23, 24, 25, 30, 37, 38, 39, 41, 51, 55, 57 (top), 59 (top), 82, 83 (top), 85 (top), 86, 87, 113 (top), 146, 148, 157 (top), 181 (bottom)
Orhan Durgut: 45
Francis Dzikowski: 152
John Feeney, courtesy of Saudi Aramco World magazine: Chapter 2-margins, 47, 67 (top), 79, 81, 89 (top)
Patrick Godeau: 63 (bottom), 65 (top and bottom)
Muhammed Görür: 43, 44
Matjaž Kačičnik: xi, xiii, 49, 69, 77 (top and bottom), 91, 95, 96, 97, 98, 99, 100, 101 (top and margin), 103, 112,116, 117,121, 123, 127, 128, 129, 131, 133 (top), 134, 135 (top), 136, 137 (top), 141 (top), 143, 150, 151 (top), 153 (top), 159, 161 (top and margin), 162,166, 167 (top and margin) 169, 171, 172, 173, 175(all), 177 (all), 179 (bottom)
Yasmine Sabry: 163 (top and margin), 165 (margin), 168, 179 (top and middle)

Line drawings by:
Ahmad Magdi and Ahmad Rabiya: 94, 133 (margin), 135 (margin), 137 (margin), 151 (margin), 153 (margin),
Jaroslaw Dobrowolski: 51, 56, 57 (margin), 80, 84, 85 (margin),
Marek Puszkarski after the survey by Antje Knuth and Michael Flechtner: 92
Marek Puszkarski: 93

Sources of reproduced material:
Description de l'Egypte ou recueil des observations et des recherches, 1822: 8, 53 (bottom), 66, 69 (bottom), 71 (top), 72, 73 (top),
Pascal Coste: *L'architecture arabe, ou Monuments du Kaire mesurés et dessinés de 1811 à 1825,* 1839: 90
Edward William Lane, *An Account of the Manners and Customs of the Modern Egyptians,* 1860: 50, 51 (margin), 59 (margin), 60, 64, 70, 83 (margin), 139 (margin), 142
David Roberts: *Egypt and Nubia,* 1846–49: 81 (margin), 145

Egyptian General Book Organisation: 61 (bottom)
Courtesy of the Historic Cairo Project: 4 (bottom), 52, 53 (top and margin), 63 (margin), 77 (margin), 89 (margin), Chapter 4 – margins, 138, 139 (top), 140, 141 (margin), 157 (margin), 158,
Library of Congress Prints and Photographs Division, Washington, D.C.: 27, 28, 32, 36, 40, 42
Courtesy of the Muhammad Mahmud Khalil Museum in Cairo: 122, 124, 125 (top and bottom),
Rijksmuseum in Amsterdam: 106, 107, 115 (margin), 118
Courtesy of the Supreme Council of Antiquities: 149, 155 (top and margin)
Topkapi Museum's collection: 10, 11 (bottom), 13, 14, 18, 20, 26, 29, 35
Wikimedia Commons: ix (right), 4 (bottom), 19 (right), 31, 33, 75 (top), 105, 108, 109, 110, 111, 113 (margin), 115 (top), 119, 147, 180
Neil Hewison's collection: 71 (top)
Authors' collection: 6, 12, 17

Quotations from Yahia Haqqi's *The Lamp of Umm Hashim* on p. 60 appear in translation by Denys Johnson-Davies (American University in Cairo Press, 2006)